THE COMPLETE BOOK OF BARBECUES

Mary Norwak

The Complete Book of Barbecues

Futura Publications Limited
A Futura Book

A Futura Book

First published in Great Britain in 1974
by Pelham Books Limited

First Futura Publications edition 1975
This edition 1978
Copyright © Mary Norwak 1974

ISBN 0 8600 72096

Printed in Great Britain by
Hazell Watson & Viney Ltd
Aylesbury, Bucks

Futura Publications Limited
110 Warner Road
Camberwell, London SE5

CONTENTS

LIST OF LINE DRAWINGS
BY SUE HOLLAND

INTRODUCTION

We have all suffered from barbecue meals where the fire is smoky, the evening is chilly, the drinks are lukewarm and the food charred outside and raw inside. Some of us, on the other hand, have enjoyed hot afternoons or warm evenings relaxing with a chilled drink and waiting for delicious food from which tempting smells are wafting.

This book is designed to help everyone to enjoy the pleasure of barbecued food. It provides an easy guide to choosing or building a barbecue, finding the right equipment, managing the fire and cooking the food. There are ideas for simple family meals, grand parties and charity barbecues, and masses of recipes which are just as good for two, twenty or two hundred guests. Just follow the easy rules, and even if you hate everyday cooking, you can enjoy preparing and eating a meal outdoors.

METRIC CONVERSION TABLE

1 ounce = 25 grammes (g)
1 pound = 500 grammes or $\frac{1}{2}$ kilogramme (kg)
1 pint = 500 millilitres (ml)
1 inch = 25 millimetres (mm) or 2·5 centimetres (cm)

OVEN TEMPERATURES

No 2 Gas = 300°F = 160°C
No 3 Gas = 325°F = 170°C
No 4 Gas = 350°F = 180°C
No 5 Gas = 375°F = 190°C
No 6 Gas = 400°F = 200°C

PART ONE

The Fire

PORTABLE BARBECUES

When you are choosing a barbecue, it is a good idea to start with a small piece of equipment. It can even be a good idea to start with an impromptu model (see 'Impromptu Barbecues') to see if this is really your style of cooking and if you and the family are prepared to cook and eat outdoors frequently. A small first model will not be wasted later if you decide to buy or build a larger barbecue, for the first one can still be used for picnics or for a supplementary fire for parties. There are many different types of barbecue on the market, and it is worth studying them carefully before buying. Good barbecues have certain points in common, but once the main requirements have been satisfied, there is still a wide choice. Work through the checklist first and then decide on the individual model.

PORTABLE BARBECUE CHECKLIST

SIZE. If there is a large family, or many guests to be catered for frequently, think about a large unit, but also consider flexibility. It may be better to have two medium-sized models, or a large and small one, to give a greater range in the number of people to be served and the kind of foods to be cooked. A secondary smaller unit can be used for beach or country picnics, or perhaps taken indoors to be used in a large fireplace with a chimney.

PORTABILITY. Models on wheels can be moved about to take advantage of wind direction, and can also be wheeled into winter storage. Models with an electric spit motor must be capable of being moved near an electrical outlet or a heavy duty extension cord. It is useful if large models can be dismantled easily for storage.

STRENGTH. Heavy gauge metals and cast iron will not warp with heat. Avoid lightweight nickel-plated wire grills, and choose chrome-plated grills for long service. See that the rods of the grills are closely spaced as this makes it easier to manage the food.

CONVENIENCE. Most people will prefer cooking at normal work height. If the barbecue only has short legs, check that you have a table, trolley or wall which will support it at the correct height. Fire-control and cooking will be more efficient if it is possible to ventilate the fire. This is usually done with a damper control. It is also important to be able to alter the distance between the food and the fire, and the mechanism for this should be easy to operate.

HOODS OR WINDSHIELDS. Although both these help to control the heat, a hood is best as it shields the top as well as the sides of the fire. It is useful to have a hood fitted with a keep-warm grill or cupboard to cope with extra supplies of food.

GRILLS. Additional folding grills and double grills with handles are useful equipment for handling delicate food. Make sure that the barbecue can accommodate extra items like these.

SPITS AND MOTORS. A motor-driven spit with battery or electrical operation is the easiest to use. It is best if this is part of the hood unit, although some spits are suspended from metal side supports or a windshield. See that spit rods and forks are strongly made. A spit basket is most useful for cooking stuffed meat or large but delicate fish which are not really held safely on the spit rod.

TOOL RACKS. On a large barbecue it is a great help to have some sort of rack for hanging cooking equipment.

ADJUSTABLE FIRES. A few very special models have fire boxes which can be altered from horizontal to vertical positions for advanced types of cooking.

TYPES OF PORTABLE BARBECUES

HIBACHI. This kind of barbecue is either round or rectangular and made in cast iron. It uses little charcoal and is very con-

venient to use in the house or on a table in the garden for small meals.

TABLE BARBECUE. A small barbecue with short legs, this can

be used in or out of doors, or can be used in a large fireplace with a chimney. It can be fitted with a spit. It is most convenient used at working height, and is suitable for small meals.

BRAZIER BARBECUE. Either round or square, this type of barbecue is fitted with legs, and sometimes wheels. Hoods and spits can be fitted to many models. Unfortunately it is often rather low for real cooking comfort.

WAGON BARBECUE. A large barbecue which is usually fitted with a pair of stable legs and a pair of legs with wheels so that

it can be moved easily. It may be fitted with a canopy, cutting and serving tables, and equipment rack, and is best suited to large parties.

PERMANENT BARBECUES

A tremendous variety of permanent barbecues can be built by an amateur or by a professional builder, both in and out of the house, but a few simple rules need to be observed for success, particularly when locating an outdoor barbecue.

INDOOR BARBECUES

A large inglenook fireplace, usually found in old houses, can be suitable for barbecueing. The original opening can be used, or a square unit with firebox can be built into the side of the opening. A barbecue fireplace can also be built into a large open porch at the front or back of the house, so that the cook is sheltered from wind or rain. Where an indoor fireplace is located on an outside wall, a barbecue can be con-

structed on the outside of the house to share the same chimney.

OUTDOOR BARBECUES

A brick-built barbecue can look attractive in a garden and be extremely practical for entertaining. Individual plans may vary considerably; some people want to incorporate an oven while others like storage or working areas, and some will only

need a simple grill above a fire box. Once the basic principles of positioning and building have been worked out, a complete individual cooking area can be devised.

LOCATION. Choose a place which looks attractive but is also practical. It is handy to be near a paved terrace, and within reach of the kitchen or garage to save a lot of carrying of food and equipment. This also ensures that there is enough light to work by, and running water for cooking and cleaning-up operations. The area should be well-drained and out of the commonly prevailing wind which will cause smoke and sparks. Keep well away from trees, shrubs, wooden or thatched buildings (at least 15 feet).

PAVED AREA. See that the fireplace can be surrounded by paving to allow people to walk about comfortably. This could be an extension of an existing terrace or a separate paved area. Allow about 3 feet to the front and sides of a small barbecue, and up to 6 feet for a large one.

FOUNDATIONS. It is important to have firm foundations which extend below the frost line. Even where an area does not catch heavy frosts, a solid foundation will prevent settling and cracks, and prevent water from creeping in.

WORKING AREA. Construct the barbecue so that the fire is easily handled and not too low. Allow for a damper adjustment to ventilate the fire, and a chimney if wood is to be burned. Have the grill at working height, allowing 6 inches clearance over a charcoal fire and 15 inches over a wood fire; adjustable grill levels are best if possible. Allow key firebricks to project slightly, or use heavy angle iron or rods, to serve as a support for the grill. Firebricks are preferable to common brick where the heat is likely to be considerable, as ordinary bricks tend to flake or break off if struck by rain or cold water while still hot. Allow room for expansion and contraction of any metal parts to prevent cracking and other damage to brickwork.

IMPROMPTU BARBECUES

There are often occasions when an improvised barbecue is needed, and a suitable fireplace can be quickly constructed in a number of ways.

BRICK BARBECUE. Form a rectangle of bricks, allowing three

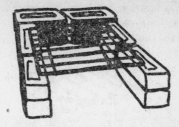

bricks down each side and four bricks at the back and front. Build up three courses of bricks, without mortar, leaving an air hole at the back and the front. Use a metal shoe-scraper, wire cake-rack or oven grid for the grill and use enough charcoal to come almost to the top of the bricks. If sloping banks of soil are built up on opposite sides of the bricks, they can be used to hold a pair of cane cross-pieces on either side, tied with wire or string; on this a thin metal rod can be supported and turned as a spit.

BRICK AND FOIL BARBECUE. Put a layer of bricks on the ground and cover it with a double thickness of aluminium foil. Anchor with two more layers of bricks on three sides. Put charcoal on the foil and cover with an oven rack, metal shoe-scraper or cake rack.

PIPE BARBECUE. Use a glazed drainage pipe with a wide end over which a circular cake rack can be fitted. A large pipe from a contractor is the right size, and you may find one that

has been abandoned because it is slightly chipped or cracked. This kind of pipe can be buried in earth or bricked in to the side of a terrace.

FLOWERPOT BARBECUE. Use a large flowerpot as a fire-holder, with a circular cake rack for a grill. A double thickness of chicken wire can be used as an improvised grill. Raise the

flowerpot on bricks to ensure a good draught for the fire.

BISCUIT TIN BARBECUE. Use a tall biscuit tin without a lid, with an oven grid or cake rack as a grill. Punch holes in the sides of the tin for ventilating the fire.

RAISED IRON BARBECUE. To get a good height for an impromptu barbecue, lay a sheet of corrugated iron between two walls, or on a few courses of bricks. On this build up one or two courses of bricks and top with a grill. Build the fire on the iron support.

WHEELBARROW BARBECUE. Put some large stones into a metal wheelbarrow to even up the bottom. Light the fire on these, and top with a grill rack extending over the sides of the wheelbarrow.

PIT BARBECUE. Dig a trench which is longer than the available metal grill and about 1 foot deep. Line with a few stones and build the fire on these. Put the grill on the earth above the pit; the extra length of trench will allow for ventilation of the fire.

FUEL

Charcoal is most commonly used for both portable and permanent barbecues, but wood can be used for permanent fireplaces and for impromptu barbecues.

CHARCOAL. Lump charcoal is cheap and easy to use and gives off a true wood smell. It catches fire quickly and burns fast. Sometimes briquettes are available, and these are clean and easy to handle, give uniform heat and a long-lasting fire, and burn without sparking. It is cheaper to buy a large sack of charcoal for storage than using very small bags which need frequent replacement.

WOOD. Soft woods such as pine, spruce, cedar and birch burn quickly and are good for starting a fire. Pine, however, can give a resinous taste to food. Hard woods such as oak, ash and beech burn more slowly and give a hotter fire, so they are better for the actual cooking. Wood for a barbecue fire should not be rotten, crumbling or damp. Aromatic woods such as fruit woods or branches of juniper bushes or bay trees can be added to the fire to give a delicious flavour to the food being cooked. Start a fire with fine twigs, pieces of bark or wood shavings, then add larger twigs, and finally logs.

ADDITIVES. Branches of aromatic woods, shrubs and herbs can be added to both charcoal and wood fires during cooking. Avoid resinous woods, or such shrubs as eucalyptus which give strong medicinal flavours to food.

LIGHTING AND MANAGING THE FIRE

The success of any barbecue depends on the skill with which the fire is managed. Not only must the fire be lit quickly, but the fuel must be brought to the correct heat before cooking and maintained at that heat. Smoke, sparks and flare-ups must be avoided, and unpleasant smells prevented.

BUILDING THE FIRE

Charcoal burns from the bottom to the top and needs bottom ventilation. Fires should be arranged to take advantage of any prevailing wind, while stiff breezes can be avoided if a hood or windshield is used. If there is a damper control on the barbecue, open it before starting the fire so that the wind blows into the opening. Once the fire has been lighted, it can be controlled by closing the damper as necessary.

If the firebox is solid, cover it with a level layer of sand or gravel (gravel is best to help give a bottom draught). This will help to protect the metal from intense heat and it will collect grease and ashes. Gravel can be washed and re-used, but it must be dry before it is used again. A lining of aluminium foil under the gravel will increase the radiant heat from the fire and help to keep the barbecue clean.

LIGHTING THE FIRE

Avoid using petrol, paraffin or grease to start a barbecue fire. They can be dangerous and will also give an unpleasant taste to food. A slow start can be made with newspaper or waxed boxes, but bellows or a fan may be needed to stimulate the fire. Firelighters can be used to start charcoal but should be used sparingly to avoid tainting the food. An electric or gas firelighter can be used if the barbecue is near the house.

Build up the fire gradually from a small start, but it is not necessary to pile on too much charcoal for successful cooking.

ARRANGING THE FIRE

When all the charcoal is burning evenly, spread it out into a cooking pattern. For normal grilling, spread the fire evenly over the whole cooking surface. For spit cooking, pile the fire about 3 inches deep behind the food on the spit and extend just underneath it.

STARTING TO COOK

A fire should be lit from 15 to 45 minutes before it is needed for cooking. It should be maintained by adding fuel to the edge of the fire, not on top of the burning charcoal. If the fire becomes very hot, old cinders from a previous barbecue can be used to cool it down. The heat should be even and glowing. A lower heat can be obtained by spacing out the fuel; greater heat can be obtained by flicking the white ash from the top of the charcoal.

To test the heat of a fire, hold your hand over it at the same distance as the food will be cooking, and count slowly until you are forced to pull your hand away from the heat. A count of 'One' means a high heat, 'Three' means medium heat and 'Five' means low heat. On a cold night, it will be more difficult to maintain a high heat, and cooking will take longer. Charcoal will also burn more slowly on a humid day.

Food should not be cooked over flames or thick smoke. The fire should be radiant; it will look grey by daylight, and glow red at night. Cooking time will depend on the heat of the fire, the distance between fire and food, and the temperature of the food when cooking begins (it should not be taken straight from the refrigerator, but should be at room temperature).

DOUSING THE FIRE

When cooking is finished, the remaining fuel need not be wasted. Douse the fire with old dried cinders from a previous barbecue. The burned charcoal can be used another time, or the ashes will provide valuable plant food for the garden. The fire can also be lifted with tongs into a water-filled bucket, then the ashes drained and dried thoroughly before re-use; a bucket of sand can be used instead. It is always important to extinguish the fire, but water should not be put directly on to the barbecue as it can damage both portable and permanent structures.

AVOIDING FIRE DAMAGE

Be sure that fires are not lit near trees, wooden buildings or dry scrubland. Consider wind direction even when you have finished cooking, as a gust of wind can rekindle charcoal. Never move a lighted barbecue if possible, and if one has to be moved, avoid going into an oncoming breeze.

Cut excess fat from meat before cooking to avoid flare-ups, and use a drip-tray for spit-roasting. Douse flames with old cinders, a water pistol, a bottle with a sprinkler top, a basting tube, a watering can, or sand. In an emergency, wet lettuce leaves will douse a small flame. Keep a small water sprinkler handy to aim at spots where these fat flare-ups occur, but do not use the water too lavishly or the heat of the fire will be reduced or totally extinguished.

PART TWO

The Basic Cooking Rules

BARBECUE EQUIPMENT

Equipment for the successful barbecue does not end with the buying or building of the actual fireplace. A small selection of tools and serving items will ease the preparations of a barbecue meal, and will ensure safety for those handling the fire. The necessary equipment need not be expensive, and most of it is already available in the kitchen. If regular barbecues are held, though, it is worth buying extra items to save loss or damage of things regularly needed for everyday meals. The barbecue equipment is best kept in a portable box or bag to save assembling items on every occasion when the fire is lit.

Avoid buying fancy or flimsy cooking tools. Be sure that everything you use is really sturdy and suitable for the tough job ahead. Otherwise, there can be some nasty accidents.

FIRE EQUIPMENT

TONGS FOR COALS. From time to time the glowing charcoal may have to be moved about. Long-handled tongs will give control over movement and allow the fire to be managed properly. Avoid pokers which may dislodge the fire and cause flare-ups; wooden sticks may also flare suddenly and cause burns.

PROTECTIVE GLOVES AND CLOTHS. An oven glove or asbestos mitten should be used constantly by those who are cooking and making the fire. This will save burns from fire or hot cooking equipment, and protect the skin from splashes of hot fat or sauce. Strong protective cloths should also be used for lifting pots and pans.

A WORKING SURFACE. This is essential for successful cooking. It is difficult and dangerous to work from floor level, so try to use a garden trolly or a folding picnic table for food and cooking equipment, as well as any serving table which may be used. Sometimes old trolleys can be found in junk shops, and when cleaned up or painted they make a useful item of barbecue furniture; the bottom shelf can be kept for the basic box of equipment, and the top used as a working surface. Heatproof mats should be placed on the surface of a wooden or plastic top.

A SPRINKLER BOTTLE OF WATER. It is important to have some water to douse flare-ups. The easiest way to handle this is with a small bottle similar to that used for sprinkling dry ironing. There are small plastic spray tops which can be used on a medicine or similar bottle.

COOKING EQUIPMENT

LONG SKEWERS. If you want to cook food on skewers, which is an easy and attractive way of serving, make sure they are long and strong. If special ones are not available, use turkey skewers. Some have fireproof handles or hand-guards for protection. Ordinary short meat skewers are not suitable for cooking food on a barbecue, but can be used for fruit or sweets for a second course which is not to be cooked.

BASTING BRUSH OR TUBE-BASTER. A small paint brush or an oven-glass tube-baster is useful for putting oil or sauce on to meats which are being cooked. If oil is poured on to the meat instead of being brushed, it can spill and flare up on the fire.

HEAVY FRYING-PAN AND SAUCEPANS WITH LONG HANDLES. Cooking pans should be strong, thick and heavy, as the heat of a barbecue fire can be intense. Plastic and wooden handles should be avoided as they may melt or char. Really long handles are essential for lifting, as short handles or loop-handles can become unbearably hot.

SHARP KNIVES. Keep a battery of sharp knives in a special box, with corks on their tips to prevent damage and injury. Have small sharp knives for cutting and trimming raw food, and a carving knife for cooked food. A spare bread knife can also be kept with the barbecue equipment.

A LONG-HANDLED FORK. This will be useful for holding food while cutting or carving. It can also be used for lifting food from the barbecue.

TONGS FOR FOOD. Many foods should not be pierced while cooking, or juices will run out. A strong pair of tongs can be used to move food on the grill and to lift foil parcels.

WOOD BOARDS. Strong chopping boards are useful for holding foods which are being prepared, and also for those which have been cooked and have to be cut and served.

WOODEN SPOONS. It is important not to use metal spoons for stirring sauces or vegetables as they quickly become very hot. Long-handled wooden spoons are the most comfortable choice.

LARGE SPOONS AND LADLES. Long-handled large spoons and ladles are useful for the serving of food. The type available on racks for kitchen use are preferable to those normally used for table service.

COOKING FOIL. This is invaluable for making parcels of food to be cooked on the grill or in the fire. It is also useful for lining tins and drip trays, and for covering food to protect it from insects. Try to have a variety of widths for different purposes.

MEAT THERMOMETER. This is not essential, but is important for spit cooking, or for large roasts. Be sure the meat thermometer is all metal, and unpainted.

COFFEE POT. A strong metal coffee pot can sit on the cooler end of the grill rack. The coffee can be made and strained into the pot to keep warm; or the pot can be a percolator in which the coffee is made over the fire.

BARBECUE SEASONINGS AND SPICES. It is worth keeping a small selection of spices, herbs and seasonings in screwtop jars in the barbecue equipment box. These can be used for sprinkling on plainly cooked meat, poultry or fish, or can be added to sauces and marinades. Fresh sprigs of herbs can be collected together just before each barbecue, but it is not always convenient to raid the kitchen each time for the other necessary flavouring ingredients.

SERVING EQUIPMENT

SERVING TABLE. While people enjoy sitting on the ground to eat their barbecue food, it is not a good idea to keep all the food on the ground as well. Food on the ground may be the prey of insects and animals, and people may tread on serving dishes. It is also extremely difficult to serve cleanly at floor level. Use a wooden garden table or trolley, an old kitchen table, or a folding picnic table.

CAN AND BOTTLE OPENERS. Keep can and bottle openers separately from those normally used in the kitchen. To avoid irritating losses at the vital moment, tie them with a cord or chain to the serving table or to a bottle basket.

BREAD BASKET. Keep a cane basket for serving bread, rolls or crispbread. They may slip from a plate or tray while being handed round. Use a large napkin or tea towel to line a basket and to cover warm bread.

ICE BUCKET. While barbecue food needs to be hot, the drinks are often nicest if served very cold. A portable ice bucket will keep ice cubes for many hours.

INSULATED CONTAINERS. There is often a long gap between starting the barbecue fire and eating the food. It is wise to store such things as salads and butter in insulated containers as protection from insects and a high temperature. An insulated picnic box or bag can be used in conjunction with a cold-pack previously chilled in the freezer or ice-making compartment of a refrigerator.

SALAD AND VEGETABLE BOWLS. Use strong bowls and serving implements for salads and vegetables, and for fruit. Wooden or stainless steel bowls are easier and safer to handle than china, glass or plastic.

PLATES, BOWLS AND GLASSES. Ordinary household crockery can be used, but disposable items are less fragile, easier to clear away, and can often be burned on the remains of a barbecue fire For small parties, or if people do not like eating from paper, you could use plastic.

CUTLERY. Fingers are often used for barbecue food, but sharp knives will be needed for steaks, and forks are handy for salads. For a large party, plastic cutlery can be used; it can be destroyed or used several times.

PAPER NAPKINS. A large supply of paper napkins is essential for mopping-up purposes. See that they are really large and strong.

ROLL OF KITCHEN PAPER. This is useful for mopping up food spills and for wrapping up bits of rubbish.

PEPPER MILL AND SALT SHAKER. These are often forgotten, but a lot of people will want to re-season their food, however carefully the cook has prepared it. Avoid small dining-room equipment, and use a really large pepper mill and salt grinder, or a bowl for the salt. Mustard, oil and vinegar or bottled sauces should also be in large, easily-handled containers.

WASTE BIN. It may seem unduly fussy to have a waste bin, but paper plates, greasy food remains, bones and salad trimmings can be quickly cleared into a small plastic dustbin with lid, or a pedal bin. This will prevent the gathering of marauding insects and food grease getting on clothes, and will make it easier to transfer rubbish to a bonfire or large dustbin.

FIRST AID EQUIPMENT

FIRST AID KIT. A motorist's first aid kit or small household kit will be suitable for use at barbecues. Sticking plasters and an antiseptic are very important to deal with small cuts. Instant aid for wasp and bee stings should be kept handy (old-fashioned but effective remedies are vinegar for wasps and bicarbonate of soda for bees).

BURN OINTMENT. Minor burns may be treated with an approved cream. This may already be included in the first aid box, but if not it can be purchased separately from a chemist.

INSECT REPELLENTS. Insects love the lights and flames of the barbecue, so keep a repellent handy. An aerosol spray is useful for a general deterrent, but sensitive skins may need a lotion.

BARBECUE CHECKLIST

1. FIRE EQUIPMENT

   (a) Tongs for coal
   (b) Protective oven gloves
   (c) Protective cloths for lifting cooking equipment
   (d) A table or other working surface near the grill
   (e) Sprinkler bottle of water to douse flames

2. COOKING EQUIPMENT

   (a) Long skewers for kebabs
   (b) Basting brush or tube-baster
   (c) Heavy frying pan with long handle
   (d) Heavy saucepans with long handles
   (e) A variety of sharp knives
   (f) Long-handled fork for holding meat while cutting and carving
   (g) Tongs for food
   (h) Wooden boards for cutting and carving
   (i) Wooden spoons for stirring sauces
   (j) Large spoons and ladles
   (k) Cooking foil
   (l) Meat thermometer
  (m) Coffee pot
   (n) Barbecue seasonings and spices

3. SERVING EQUIPMENT

- (a) Serving table
- (b) Can and bottle openers
- (c) Bread basket
- (d) Ice bucket
- (e) Insulated containers
- (f) Salad and vegetable bowls with serving spoons and forks
- (g) Plates, bowls and glasses (paper or plastic for easy clearing)
- (h) Cutlery
- (i) Paper napkins
- (j) Roll of kitchen paper
- (k) Pepper mill and salt shaker
- (l) Waste bin

4. FIRST AID EQUIPMENT

- (a) First aid kit
- (b) Burn ointment
- (c) Insect repellents

COOKING TIMES

There is great skill in cooking meat correctly on the barbecue grill. The correct degree of 'doneness' depends on the weight and thickness of the food being cooked, and on the distance between the grill and the fire. To achieve varying degrees of cooked meat, the distance between the grill and the fire should be altered.

Any meat being cooked should be grilled on both sides on a ready-heated grill, and should not be pierced with a fork or knife since flavour-holding juices will be lost. White meat should be very thin and well-cooked; beef should be no thicker than $1\frac{1}{2}$ inches and can be cooked to taste. This means that white meat should be cooked slowly towards the edge of the fire when it has reached the hot stage with white ash.

Red meat should be cooked close to the centre of the grill over a red hot fire. Red meat is usually enjoyed in four different stages of cooking:

RARE OR BLUE. The outside looks lightly brown while the centre is bright red and practically raw.

UNDERDONE. The outside should be golden brown, and the meat should look cooked almost through. In the centre there should be a strip of light red meat with a slight drop of blood visible.

MEDIUM. The outside should be a good brown, with the centre pinkish turning towards light tan.

WELL DONE. The outside should be a very dark brown and the centre light brown.

COOKING TIME CHART

ITEM	SIZE OR WEIGHT	COOKING TIME (MINUTES) EACH SIDE				SPECIAL NOTES
		Rare	*Under-done*	*Medium*	*Well done*	
BEEF						
Skewer		4	6-8	8-10	12	Beef is best
Steak	1 in thick	5	7	8	10	served rare
	1½ ins thick	6	8	10	12	or under-
	2 ins thick	8	10	15	20	done
	2½ ins thick	12	15	18	25	
Burgers	1 in thick	4	5	6	7	
LAMB						
Skewer				8	10	Lamb may
Chops	1 in thick	4-5	6	6-7	8	be cooked
	1½ ins thick	5-6	7	8-9	10	rare if
	2 ins thick	6-7	8	9-10	12	preferred
PORK						
Skewer					13	Pork
Chops	1 in thick				13-18	should be
	1½ ins thick				15-23	well done
	2 ins thick				20-30	but juicy
Spare ribs	Whole rack				1-1½ hours altogether	Turn often

ITEM	SIZE OR WEIGHT	COOKING TIME (MINUTES) EACH SIDE				SPECIAL NOTES
		Rare	Under-done	Medium	Well done	
VEAL Skewer					15	Veal should
Chops	1 in				9-10	be well
	1½ ins				12-15	done but not dry
POULTRY Chicken Pieces					30-40 altogether	
Whole Chicken on Spit	per lb				30	
Duck (split)					25	
HAM Slices	1 in thick				15-18	
	1½ ins thick				18-23	
FISH Fillets	Small				3-6	Do not
	Large				6-9	overcook or
Steaks	1 in thick				3-5	fish will be
	1½ ins thick				4-6	dry
Whole	per ½ lb				20	
Fresh sardines					6	

PLANNING BARBECUE MENUS

While a barbecue is meant to be an impromptu and carefree way of preparing meals, like all ad libs it needs careful preparation. A barbecue needs as careful planning as a dinner party if the family and guests are going to enjoy something more than a bit of charred chicken, a bursting sausage and a lettuce leaf.

SUITING THE OCCASION

The barbecue menu must be planned according to the type

of guests, the tastes of the family, and the sort of party you intend to give bearing in mind the budget and the kind of food currently available. You may just want a simply family lunch or supper, or a spontaneous gathering of a few close friends. On the other hand, you may be entertaining a children's party, raising money for charity, or organising a full-scale full-dress party. The menu for each occasion will have the same basic outline, but will differ widely in its components. This is dealt with more fully in Part Four.

THE OUTLINE MENU

Any barbecue meal must centre round its main course, whether this is to be meat, poultry or fish. The successful meal, however, will be built up on this basis, with a suitable starting course, appropriate vegetables and/or salads, sauces, breads, sweet course and drinks. As in planning all good meals, the question of contrasts should be carefully considered, with due attention given to flavour, texture and colour. Full suggestions and recipes are given in Part Three.

FIRST COURSES

For any type of party and for any age-group, a first course is essential. There can be a very long interval indeed between lighting the fire and providing the food, and something to nibble while waiting and sipping drinks is important. This can be of the simplest kind, such as potato crisps and salted nuts, or creamy dips with raw vegetables for dunking. Pâté of various kinds with crispbread or biscuits is a good idea, and seafood makes delicious appetisers if fish is not the main course. On a rather chilly night, a mug of hot clear soup may be welcome.

MAIN COURSES

The main course will depend very much on circumstances and the budget. Children usually prefer plenty of sausages and burgers. A family lunch may be juickly planned around the meat, poultry or fish which has already been bought for an indoor meal. Chicken pieces are probably the most economical purchase for a large party. Money-no-object parties can be planned around large steaks, joints on the spit, poultry cooked whole, salmon or trout.

VEGETABLES AND SALADS

The easiest accompaniment is a green or tomato salad, with crisps. For a party, a selection of salads will be needed. Potatoes in their jackets are popular and all types of vegetables can be cooked in foil. It is also possible, of course, to use heavy saucepans to cook vegetables in the conventional manner, and potatoes can be fried in shallow fat in a thick pan.

SAUCES AND MARINADES

A variety of sauces and marinades will give succulence and flavour to all barbecue cooking. Bottled sauces can be used, or special recipes can be prepared.

BREADS

Bread is an important part of the barbecue menu, not only to fill corners for hungry appetites, but also for mopping up sauces and meat juices. For first courses and initial nibbling, a basket of assorted crispbreads, oatcakes and bread sticks can be used, and these will also come in handy if cheese is to be served later. Crusty long loaves are the most popular for general service, and are all the better if served hot and flavoured with garlic or other herbs. Don't forget plenty of fresh, firm butter to go with it.

SWEET COURSES

Some people will only want cheese and fresh fruit such as

apples. For a more elaborate meal, bowls of soft fruit in season, sugared and with cream, are refreshing. Large open fruit flans or simple gateaux are good for parties. Children like fruit and marshmallows heated on skewers, perhaps with a chocolate sauce to dip into. If it can be kept cold, ice cream and a variety of sauces will provide a sweet ending. Avoid mousses, cold sweet soufflés, fruit fools, or anything which becomes messy when served outdoors and is difficult to eat.

DRINKS

For the family, beer, cider and soft drinks will be the most popular. For a party, the same drinks can be supplemented by spirits or a variety of aperitifs; wine or a mixed cup can be served with the meal. Plenty of hot strong coffee will be enjoyed at leisure after the main cooking and eating is over. If the party is a long one, mugs of soup can be served from the barbecue fire at going-home time. Children will enjoy soft drinks, milk drinks or hot chocolate.

QUANTITIES

It is hopeless to be mean with barbecue food because appetites are sharpened by the open air, by the necessary wait for food, by preliminary drinking, and by the 'come-again' atmosphere encouraged by the sight of food cooking. It is probably a fairly safe rule to think of average indoor helpings and then to double them.

PRE-COOKED FOOD AND FOOD FROM THE FREEZER

If a large party is planned, it is wise to prepare some of the food beforehand, either to a completed stage, or ready for reheating.

PRE-COOKED FOOD

Steaks and fish are spoiled by reheating, but poultry joints can be carefully prepared for final browning, and this is useful for a really large party. If you do not do some pre-cooking, several people will be waiting for their food hours after others have finished.

CHICKEN PIECES. Put these into oven trays. Brush lightly with oil, and sprinkle with salt, pepper and a little barbecue spice. Cook in the oven at 375°F (Gas Mark 5) for 40 minutes, basting with the pan juices once during cooking. Drain off the pan juices. These can be used for basting sauces or for soups. Cool the chicken pieces and keep in the refrigerator until needed. This pre-cooking could be done on the morning of a barbecue party, or on the day before the party. To finish off the cooking, the pieces should be put on the barbecue grill, brushed with oil or sauce and a sprinkling of herbs, and grilled until brown and crisp on the outside.

SAUSAGES. These can take up a lot of room on the grill. For a large party, cook them in trays in the oven, or under the kitchen grill. Put on oven trays at the side of the barbecue grill to keep warm, or spread out on the grill for a final browning and crisping.

LAMB OR PORK CHOPS. The same method can be used for large quantities of chops for a party, leaving the barbecue grill clear for other items. These can be brushed with a sauce for finishing on the grill over charcoal.

FIRST COURSES AND SWEET COURSES. It is sensible to prepare appetisers, first courses and sweet courses in advance and keep them under refrigeration or in the freezer until needed. Salads may also be prepared beforehand and kept chilled. Ice cream can be stored in the freezer, together with sweet sauces. These can also be kept in the refrigerator, and so can whipped or pouring cream.

FOOD FROM THE FREEZER

The freezer can play a useful double part in preparations for a barbecue. In addition to storing ready-prepared first courses and sweet courses, it is also invaluable for keeping in stock the raw materials of an outdoor meal. When the weather has decided to be kind, it is often too late to shop for an impromptu meal. In addition to supplies of steak, chops, chicken pieces and sausages, vegetables and bread can be stored. Supplies of burgers and fish fingers are useful for quick meals for children. Bulk supplies of ice cream are quickly available from the freezer, and commercially-prepared iced cakes, coffee cakes and cheesecakes are useful for quick sweet courses.

KEEPING FOOD AND DRINK HOT OR COLD

There is nothing nastier—or even more dangerous—than lukewarm food or drink. Barbecue food should be piping hot, while appropriate accompaniments and drinks should be thoroughly chilled. It is also important that raw food such as meat, poultry and fish should be kept cold and covered until used.

KEEPING FOOD HOT

For a small party, food can be kept hot at the side of the barbecue grill. For a larger party, a second (or even third) barbecue fire can be used just to keep food hot while further quantities are being cooked. A covering of foil or a lid on pans will help to keep food warm.

It is a good idea, if space is limited on the barbecue, to use a candle-warmer on the serving table to keep some items hot; a portable chafing-dish is also useful for sauces or dips. If the barbecue is held on a terrace near the house, an electric food-warmer at an open window can be used.

If there are large quantities of foil-wrapped items, such as bread or potatoes, to be kept warm, try putting these in a version of the old hay-box. Use a packing case or thick cardboard box, and line it with an old, thick blanket. Fill it with hay or straw. Wrap the foil-covered food in a parcel of old blanket or a towel, and bury them in the hay. Cover with hay and put on a lid and they will keep hot for a long time.

KEEPING FOOD AND DRINK COLD

Keep cold food and drink really well chilled in the refrigerator until the last possible minute before serving. Transfer drinks and even bowls of fruit to baths or tubs of ice. Large quantities of ice can be made in meat trays or polythene bags in the freezer. Serve seafood and salads from bowls standing in larger bowls of crushed ice. Use an ice bucket for cubes to add to drinks. Keep an insulated box or bag with a chilled cold-bag handy for extra quantities of food and for butter, cream, runny cheeses and so on.

FLAVOURING WITH HERBS, SPICES AND SEASONINGS

Complementary flavourings are very important in a barbecue meal. While plainly grilled meat or fish may be delicious, it will be even better if cooked with the right blends of herbs, spices or seasonings. The keen barbecue cook will like to keep a separate container of favourite flavourings with the barbecue equipment, and it is worth assembling a small herb and spice box, and a rack of useful sauces. These can be used in a variety of ways for main course dishes, salads and vegetables.

HERBS

Sprinkle fresh or dried herbs on cooked meat, poultry or fish, and add them to salads and vegetables. During the main barbecue season, fresh herbs will be available and should be used whenever possible. If possible, sprinkle the meat or poultry to be cooked with herbs 24 hours before cooking. A few aromatic herbs scattered over the charcoal while cooking will give a delicious flavour to the food, and the scent will stimulate appetites. A bunch of herbs such as bay leaves, rosemary, thyme or marjoram will add a delicate flavour if used for brushing on oil.

HERB CHECKLIST

BASIL. Particularly good in tomato salad. Use sparingly with lamb, liver, poultry, fish, seafood.

BAY. Use in marinades, or as a basting brush. Good with ham, pork and poultry.

CARAWAY. Sprinkle lightly on pork or veal. Good with cabbage salads. Sprinkle on bread or rolls before heating.

CELERY SEED. Use in salad dressings and marinades. Good with chicken and ham, or to spike up tomato juice.

CHERVIL. Delicious with chicken, fish, mushrooms, and new potatoes.

CHIVES. Sprinkle on salads or on jacket potatoes.

DILL. Use with potatoes, cucumber salad or fish.

FENNEL. Use for fish.

GARLIC. Chop or crush garlic cloves for marinades and barbecue sauces. Wipe round a salad bowl for extra flavour. Use to make hot garlic bread.

MARJORAM. A member of the Origanum family (Oregano can be substituted, but has a strong flavour). Use in salads, sauces for fish, and as a flavour-aid for grilled pork, veal, lamb or liver, or fish.

MINT. Use with lamb, with new potatoes or peas, and with tomato or green salads. Also good chopped finely in a fruit salad.

PARSLEY. Chop and sprinkle over vegetables and salads. Use with fish, chicken and bacon or ham.

ROSEMARY. Good for fish, lamb, beef, pork, veal. Brush off before serving as the spikes can be irritating.

SAGE. Rather a powerful flavour, but good with veal, liver, sausages and burgers.

SAVORY. Use for poultry and fish.

TARRAGON. For lamb, pork and chicken, and fish. Use with melted butter on steak. Add to salad dressings.

THYME. Use with pork, veal, lamb or beef, or poultry. Sprinkle over cooked vegetables.

BOUQUET GARNI. A mixture of thyme, parsley and bay leaves, to which marjoram, basil or sage are sometimes added. Useful for marinades, plus a tiny piece of dried orange peel.

HERBES DE PROVENCE. Very aromatic herbs from the South of France, consisting of some of the above varieties, and excellent for barbecue use.

POULTRY STUFFING. If herbs are not quickly available for impromptu use, packeted poultry stuffing may be used to sprinkle on grilled meat, poultry or fish, or it can be lightly stirred into barbecue sauces.

COOKING CHECKLIST

If choice is limited, use these easily obtained herbs for basic cooking.

Meat or fish	Herb
Beef	*Rosemary, savory*
Lamb	*Thyme, rosemary*
Veal	*Thyme*
Pork	*Sage*
Poultry and game	*Thyme*
Fish	*Fennel*

SPICES AND SEASONINGS

A number of common spices and seasonings are used in barbecue cookery, but there are some additional blended seasonings and sauces which save keeping a large supply of ingredients, and which give the correct hot spicy flavour to charcoal-grilled food.

BARBECUE SEASONING. This is a specially blended powder which will give a 'lift' to all grilled meats, poultry and fish, and can be added to sauces.

CAYENNE PEPPER. This is a very hot pepper to be used sparingly; it is often added to seafood dishes.

CELERY SALT. This gives the taste of celery to sauces and salad dressings, but beware of adding extra salt as well.

CHILLI POWDER. Another very hot seasoning. Use sparingly in burgers, or other dishes made with minced beef.

GARLIC POWDER. An easy way to add a touch of garlic to all kinds of dishes.

GARLIC SALT. Another way of giving a garlic flavour, but again this adds extra salt to a dish

ITALIAN SEASONING. Good with vegetables and fish, and particularly with tomatoes, as it has a strong flavour of herbs.

MUSTARD. Many varieties now available. A basic collection would consist of English, French and German, but many individual recipes from these countries can now be obtained. Use in salad dressings, as well as with steak, pork and poultry.

ONION POWDER. Useful for giving onion flavouring if only a little is required.

ONION SALT. Another way of adding onion flavour, but very salty.

PEPPER. Freshly ground black pepper is best for barbecues.

POULTRY SEASONING. Another blended seasoning with plenty of herbs which is good with poultry and also with pork and veal.

SALT. Use ground rock salt or flakes of sea salt for the best flavour.

STEAK SEASONING. A blended seasoning which is particularly suitable for red meat.

TABASCO. A very hot pepper sauce. Add just a few drops to sauces; particularly good in seafood dishes.

WORCESTERSHIRE SAUCE. Another hot sauce, to be used sparingly in barbecue sauces. Particularly good with beef dishes.

PART THREE

The Food

'It is probably a fairly safe rule to think of average indoor helpings and then to double them.'

FIRST COURSES

As we have already seen, there may be a long wait before the main course, so guests should be given some food to nibble with drinks, to take the edge off keen appetites. A barbecue first course should be appetising and fairly light, and easily handled in the fingers. Seafood is particularly appetising before an outdoor meal, but pâtés and dips are also popular. They can be prepared beforehand, and served with a variety of breads, biscuits and crispbreads.

CRUDITÉS

Carrots
Celery
Small tomatoes
Green and red peppers
Cucumbers

Spring onions
Cauliflowers
Button mushrooms
Chicory
Radishes

Use very fresh, crisp vegetables. Cut carrots, celery, peppers, and cucumbers into strips. Use only the flowerets of the cauliflowers. Leave tomatoes, spring onions, mushrooms and radishes whole. Separate the chicory into leaves. Arrange in bowls or on wide platters. Serve with sea salt, a pepper mill of black pepper, a dish of unsalted butter, or a dip

CRAB SNACKS

1 lb crabmeat (fresh, frozen
or canned)
Worcestershire sauce
Tabasco sauce

Mayonnaise
Salt and pepper
Streaky bacon

Mix together crabmeat with sauces, mayonnaise and seasoning to taste. Only a few drops of Worcestershire and Tabasco sauces will be needed, but there should be enough mayonnaise to bind the crabmeat firmly. Form the crab into small balls and wrap each in a thin piece of bacon. Fix with cocktail sticks and grill or fry until bacon is crisp and brown. These are best prepared in the kitchen, although they can be carefully threaded on to skewers to cook over the barbecue.

PICKLED PRAWNS

1 lb peeled prawns   *1 tablespoon capers*
4 oz onions   *1 teaspoon celery seed*
4 bay leaves   *½ teaspoon salt*
6 fl oz salad oil   *Few drops of Tabasco sauce*
3 fl oz white wine vinegar

Arrange the prawns, thinly sliced onions and bay leaves in a dish. Mix together the remaining ingredients and pour into the dish. Cover and refrigerate for 24 hours, spooning the liquid over the fish occasionally. Drain and serve prawns on cocktail sticks.

SEAFOOD AND MUSHROOM SALAD

1 lb button mushrooms   *Lemon juice*
8 scallops   *1 clove crushed garlic*
4 oz prawns   *Salt and pepper*
Olive oil   *Chopped parsley*

Wipe the mushrooms and slice them fairly thinly. Cover with olive oil and add a squeeze of lemon juice, the garlic, salt and pepper. Simmer the scallops in a little salted water; cooking the white fish for 5 minutes but only adding the red coral for the last minute. Drain them, and cut each scallop into 2 rounds. While still warm, mix with the prawns and season with salt, pepper and a little lemon juice. Just before serving, mix the fish and mushrooms together and garnish with parsley. This is a refreshing and unusual first course which is excellent before a large and highly-spiced barbecue main course.

CRAB AND CHEESE DIP

2 oz Danish Blue cheese
2 oz cream cheese
½ teaspoon Worcestershire sauce

1 clove crushed garlic
1 teaspoon lemon juice
6 oz fresh or tinned crab-meat

Blend together cheeses and gradually work in sauce, crushed garlic, lemon juice and crabmeat. Pile into bowl. Serve with crisps, raw vegetable sticks or bread sticks.

HAM AND HORSERADISH DIP

8 oz cooked ham
1 tablespoon chopped parsley

1 tablespoon grated horse-radish
4 oz cream cheese

Put ham through mincer and blend in parsley, horseradish and cream cheese. Serve in a bowl surrounded by crisps or small salted biscuits.

ORANGE CHEESE DIP

4 oz cream cheese
1 tablespoon grated orange rind

¼ teaspoon salt
Pinch of paprika

Blend together cheese, orange rind, salt and paprika. Serve with crisps.

CHICKEN LIVER PÂTÉ

8 oz chicken livers
3 oz fat bacon
2 cloves crushed garlic

1 small onion
1 egg
Salt and pepper

Cut livers in small pieces and chop bacon and onion. Cook bacon and onion in a little butter until onion is just soft. Add livers and cook gently for 10 minutes. Mince very finely and season. Add garlic and beaten egg, and put mixture into foil containers or ovenproof dishes. Stand containers in a baking tin of water and cook at 350°F (Gas Mark 4) for 1 hour. Cool completely. Serve with crispbread.

COD'S ROE PÂTÉ

> *12 oz smoked cod's roe*
> *1 gill double cream*
> *1 clove crushed garlic*

> *Juice of ½ lemon*
> *1 dessertspoon olive oil*
> *Black pepper*

Scrape roe into bowl and mix to a smooth paste with cream, garlic, lemon, oil and pepper. Pack into small containers. Serve with crispbread.

KIPPER PÂTÉ

> *6 oz frozen buttered kipper fillets*   *Pepper and nutmeg*
> *1½ oz softened butter*

Cook fillets as directed on packet, and turn contents including juices into a bowl. Remove fish skin, and mince or pound kipper and juices finely. Beat in soft butter and season to taste with pepper and nutmeg. Serve with crispbread.

PORK PÂTÉ

> *¾ lb pig's liver*
> *2 lb pork belly*
> *1 large onion*
> *1 large egg*

> *1 tablespoon flour*
> *Salt, pepper and nutmeg*
> *Parsley*
> *Streaky bacon*

Put liver and pork through coarse mincer. Chop onion and soften in a little butter. Mix together meat, onion, egg beaten with flour, seasoning and a little chopped parsley. Line foil dish, terrine or loaf tin with rashers of streaky bacon flattened with a knife. Put in mixture. Cover with greaseproof paper and lid, and stand container in a baking tin of water. Cook at 350°F (Gas Mark 4) for 1½ hours. Cool under weights. Serve with crispbread.

MEAT AND POULTRY

The barbecue is usually associated with grilled food, and most people start with cooking by this method before experimenting with spit, foil or skewer cooking. To achieve perfection in barbecue grilling, it is important to select meat carefully, and to pay a little attention to basic grilling rules.

CHOOSING MEAT

BEEF. Good quality prime cuts are best for grilling, as they should be tender and of good flavour. Sirloin, rump and fillet are most commonly used, but chuck steak is suitable if marinaded first. The best meat should be marbled with fat which will make it tender when cooked. Excess fat on the outside of the meat should be trimmed to avoid flare-ups on the barbecue. If meat is very lean, it will lack flavour, and tend to be tough. About 7 oz per person should be allowed for steaks, but the meat may cook better and taste more delicious if it is cooked in one large piece and then carved into slices (see 'Successful Grilling').

LAMB. Lamb is excellent for barbecue grilling. Flesh will vary from light pink to light or dark red, according to the age and type of animal. Look for creamy white fat, rather than that which is brittle and yellowish. A little oil will help in cooking, and a variety of herbs give extra flavour to the meat.

PORK. Pork chops and lean slices from the top of the leg are good for the barbecue, and slices of belly pork can also be grilled. Spare ribs of pork are popular, although messy. See that the meat is firm, smooth and fresh. It should be pink, with little gristle but some small specks of fat. Ham and thick slices of bacon are also useful for the barbecue.

VEAL. The meat should be soft and moist, but never wet or flabby. It should be pale pink or almost white, with a fine texture. As there will be little fat, the meat can be dry for grilling.

POULTRY. Use fresh or frozen poultry, but make sure that any frozen bird has been completely defrosted before cooking.

SUCCESSFUL GRILLING

The grill should be hot before food is put on to it, and it

must be large enough to accommodate the food comfortably. It should be oiled to prevent food sticking. Be sure to time the cooking of food carefully (see page 24), according to its size and thickness, and cook both sides of meat or poultry.

THIN CUTS OF MEAT. About 1½ inches is the correct thickness for meat, although white meat can be cut thinner and needs to be well-cooked. Red meat is best cooked in the centre of the grill, close to the heat, but white meat may be cooked more slowly at the edge of the fire when it has reached the white ash stage. It is important not to pierce meat with a knife or fork during cooking, as juices will be lost. If meat is turned frequently during cooking, the juices will circulate and the meat will remain moist and full of flavour.

LARGE STEAKS. For a party of people, a large piece of steak (allowing 7-8 oz per portion) can be cooked over slow heat, which may take up to 2 hours, with frequent turning. The meat can then be removed to a carving platter and cut into thick slices.

THE PERFECT STEAK

It is an art to cook the perfect steak, but well worth taking a little extra trouble. Score the edges of the meat so that it will not curl up, and trim outer rim of fat. When the fire is blazing hot, tap off the grey ash with tongs. As soon as the grill rods are hot, grease them and put on the steaks. When little bubbles come to the top surface of the meat, turn carefully with tongs. Grill to the exact time suggested for 'doneness' required. Do not salt steak before cooking, or the juices will be drawn out, and so will the flavour. Salt and pepper each side as it is sealed by the heat, and serve steaks very hot. If you like a charcoal flavour and a dark crusty coating, lower the grill very close to the fire for 2 minutes and then return to normal position to cook that side. Repeat the process to brown the other side before finishing cooking.

FRIED GARLIC STEAKS

   6 minute steaks   *1 tablespoon Worcester-*
   2 oz butter   *shire sauce*
   1 clove crushed garlic   *Salt and pepper*
   Juice of 1 lemon

This is a good way to use minute steaks from the freezer, as they are often very thin and lean and unsuitable for grilling. Use a heavy frying pan on the grill over a hot fire. Melt the butter and add the crushed garlic. Dip steaks in the butter to coat them, and cook them for 2 minutes on each side. Add the lemon juice and Worcestershire sauce to the pan, mixing them well with the pan juices. Move steaks through this sauce and serve them on slices of toasted French bread to catch the juices. The steaks can be seasoned to taste with salt and pepper as they are served.

STEAKS WITH WINE

   4 grilling steaks   *3 tablespoons olive oil*
   5 fl oz dry white wine   *Salt and pepper*
   2 small onions   *Breadcrumbs*
   2 sprigs tarragon

Mix together the wine, chopped onions, tarragon, salt and pepper, and oil. Leave the steaks in this mixture for 1 hour. Grill steaks for 3 minutes each side. Remove from the grill and coat with breadcrumbs. Continue grilling over high heat, brushing with marinade while cooking.

HERB STEAKS

   4 grilling steaks   *1 tablespoon chopped*
   4 tablespoons vinegar   *chervil*
   8 tablespoons olive oil   *1 tablespoon chopped*
   2 small onions   *chives*
   4 cloves crushed garlic *Salt and pepper*
   1 tablespoon chopped
     parsley

Mix together vinegar, oil, sliced onions, garlic and herbs.

Leave the steaks in the mixture for 1 hour. Season with salt and pepper and put on the grill over medium heat. Brush with the marinade during cooking.

GRILLED CHUCK STEAK

2 lb chuck steak	¼ teaspoon pepper
1 medium onion	Pinch of thyme
4 fl oz lemon juice	Pinch of marjoram
2 fl oz salad oil	Pinch of rosemary
¼ teaspoon salt	1 clove crushed garlic
¼ teaspoon celery salt	

Cut the chuck steak in ½ inch slices. Chop the onion finely. Mix with lemon juice, salad oil, salt, celery salt, pepper, herbs and crushed garlic. Cover the meat with this mixture and leave in a refrigerator for 3 hours, turning the meat several times. Drain off the marinade, saving it for basting. Grill over a hot fire, basting often.

VEAL CHOPS WITH KIRSCH

4 veal chops	2 fl oz kirsch
1 fl oz olive oil	Juice of 1 orange
Salt and pepper	Chopped parsley

Brush the chops with the oil and season well on both sides with the salt and pepper. Grill on both sides over high heat. Put on to a hot dish, pour on the kirsch and set light to it. Add the orange juice and sprinkle with parsley.

HERBED LAMB STEAKS

4 slices leg of lamb	2 cloves crushed garlic
6 fl oz olive oil	Sprig of rosemary
4 tablespoons chopped fresh mixed herbs	Salt and pepper

Mix together the oil, herbs, garlic, rosemary, salt and pepper. Leave the meat in this marinade for 1 hour. Put meat on the grill and cook over medium heat, brushing with the marinade while cooking.

LAMB CUTLETS WITH CHEESE

8 lamb cutlets
2 eggs
Pepper

4 oz grated Gruyère cheese
Dry breadcrumbs

Beat the eggs with pepper. Dip in the cutlets and cover them with cheese and breadcrumbs. Grill over medium heat.

LAMB CHOPS WITH CHEESE

6 lamb chops (1 inch thick)
2 oz grated Parmesan
cheese

2 tablespoons softened
butter
Salt and pepper

Grill the chops over medium heat for 5 minutes on each side. Mix cheese, butter, salt and pepper and spread on the chops. Continue grilling for 2 minutes.

MARINADED LAMB CHOPS

8 thick lamb chops
8 fl oz tomato juice
4 fl oz lemon juice
1 large onion
1 green pepper

½ teaspoon salt
½ teaspoon black pepper
½ teaspoon cumin
½ teaspoon marjoram

Mix together the tomato and lemon juices, finely chopped onion and green pepper, salt and pepper, cumin and marjoram. Pour over the lamb chops and leave to stand for 4 hours. Drain the chops and grill them slowly about 20 minutes each side, basting occasionally with the marinade. Heat the remaining marinade to serve as a sauce.

HERBED PORK CHOPS

4 pork chops
Sprig of sage
Sprig of thyme
Bay leaves

6 tablespoons olive oil
Squeeze of lemon juice
Salt and pepper

Mix together the herbs, oil, lemon juice and seasoning. Soak the meat in this marinade for 1 hour. Grill over medium heat, brushing with the marinade during cooking.

SPARERIBS IN BARBECUE SAUCE

4 lb meaty spareribs	8 fl oz water
8 fl oz bottled sauce	1 dessertspoon sugar
1 dessertspoon Worcester-	½ teaspoon salt
shire sauce	½ teaspoon celery seed
3 drops Tabasco sauce	1 lemon
2 fl oz vinegar	1 medium onion

Spareribs should be tender and juicy inside with a crisp brown outside; the lean should show no pinkness when cut. The meat should be cooked very slowly for a long time, with frequent turning. It may be more practical to roast the spareribs for 1 hour at 350°F (Gas Mark 4) in the kitchen, before finishing on the barbecue. Sprinkle them with salt first. Mix together the bottled sauce, Worcestershire sauce, Tabasco sauce, water, vinegar, sugar, salt, and celery seed, and simmer for 30 minutes. Brush the ribs with this sauce and cover with thin slices of lemon and onion. Cook for 30-40 minutes until done, brushing often with the sauce.

SPICED ORANGE GLAZED SPARERIBS

3 lb meaty spareribs	Juice of 2 oranges
Marinade and glaze	2 tablespoons Worcester-
2 tablespoons clear honey	shire sauce
Juice of ½ lemon	1 teaspoon soy sauce
Finely grated rind of ½	Salt
orange	

Combine all marinade ingredients in a pan and heat gently. Simmer for 2 minutes. Cool. Cut spareribs into serving pieces and place in a shallow dish. Pour over marinade and leave for 12-24 hours, turning occasionally. Remove spareribs and place in a roasting pan. Keep marinade. Roast spareribs at 350°F (Gas Mark 4) for 1 hour. When required place on top of barbecue grill and brush well with marinade. Cook, turning frequently and brushing with marinade, for about 10-15 minutes until well-glazed and crisp.

BARBECUED HAM

1½ lb cooked ham cut ½
   inch thick
6 fl oz bottled sauce
1½ tablespoons brown sugar
1 tablespoon French
   mustard

1 tablespoon Worcester-
   shire sauce
1 tablespoon lemon juice
3 drops Tabasco sauce

Slash the edges of the ham to prevent curling. Cook the ham in two or three slices. Mix together the bottled sauce, brown sugar, mustard, Worcestershire sauce, lemon juice and Tabasco sauce and cover the ham with this, leaving it for 1 hour. Grill 5 minutes each side, brushing well with the sauce.

PINEAPPLE AND ORANGE HAM

1½ lb cooked ham cut 1
   inch thick
2 fl oz orange juice
2 fl oz sherry

½ teaspoon mustard powder
Pinch of mixed herbs
4 canned pineapple slices

Mix together the orange juice, sherry, mustard and herbs and brush over the ham. Grill over a hot fire for 7 minutes each side, basting often. Just before cooking finishes, grill the pineapple slices for 2 minutes each side, basting often with the sauce.

DEVILLED CHICKEN

4 large chicken pieces
1 dessertspoon salt
1 dessertspoon sugar
1 teaspoon pepper
1 teaspoon ground ginger
1 teaspoon dry mustard
½ teaspoon curry powder
2 oz butter

2 tablespoons tomato sauce
1 tablespoon mushroom
   ketchup
1 tablespoon Worcester-
   shire sauce
1 tablespoon soy sauce
1 tablespoon plum jam
4 drops Tabasco sauce

Put the chicken pieces in a shallow dish. Mix together the salt, sugar, pepper, ginger, mustard and curry powder and cover the chicken thoroughly with the mixture. Leave for 1 hour. Melt the butter and brush over the chicken pieces. Grill for 10 minutes over medium heat on each side until brown and crisp. Mix the tomato sauce, mushroom ketchup, Worcestershire sauce, soy sauce, plum jam, and Tabasco sauce together with any remaining butter. Heat gently and use to baste the chicken continually during further cooking (about 7 minutes each side). Use remaining sauce to serve with the chicken.

BARBECUED CHICKEN

4 large chicken pieces	*1 dessertspoon Worcester-*
8 fl oz tomato sauce	*shire sauce*
4 fl oz water	*1 teaspoon mustard powder*
2 tablespoons black treacle	*½ teaspoon salt*
1 tablespoon butter	*Shake of pepper*
1 tablespoon vinegar	*4 drops Tabasco sauce*
1 small onion	

This can be prepared in the kitchen beforehand. Use a heavy saucepan, and mix together the tomato sauce, water, treacle, butter, vinegar, finely chopped onion, Worcestershire sauce, mustard, salt and pepper, and Tabasco sauce. Simmer for 20 minutes. Brush the chicken pieces with salad oil and grill over low heat for 20 minutes, bone side down. Turn and grill for 15 minutes. Brush with the sauce and continue grilling for about 15 minutes, turning the chickens occasionally and basting with the sauce.

PINEAPPLE GLAZED CHICKEN

4 large chicken pieces	*8 oz can crushed pineapple*
4 fl oz salad oil	*6 oz brown sugar*
1 teaspoon salt	*1 tablespoon lemon juice*
¼ teaspoon pepper	*1 tablespoon made mustard*

Brush the chicken pieces well with oil and season with salt and pepper. Grill over a slow fire, starting with the bone side down, for 20 minutes on each side. Drain the pineapple but keep 1 tablespoon pineapple syrup. Mix the pineapple, the reserved syrup, brown sugar, lemon juice, mustard and a pinch of salt. Brush this over both sides of the chicken pieces. Grill 10 minutes more, turning the chicken pieces often and brushing well with the pineapple glaze. Serve any remaining glaze as a sauce.

SPRING CHICKENS AND MUSTARD

4 spring chickens	*1 teaspoon thyme*
1 fl oz olive oil	*1 teaspoon rosemary*
1 tablespoon French mustard	*2 bay leaves*
	Salt and pepper

Split the chickens in two, open them out and flatten them. Mix together the oil, mustard, thyme, rosemary, crushed bay leaves, and salt and pepper. Brush over the chickens and put them bone side down on the grill. Grill for 15 minutes, then turn them and cook for 20 minutes.

BARBECUED FRANKFURTERS

1 medium onion	*3 tablespoons sweet stout*
2 tablespoons salad oil	*3 tablespoons vinegar or lemon juice*
2 teaspoons sugar	
¾ teaspoon dry mustard	*2 teaspoons Worcestershire sauce*
¼ teaspoon salt	
⅛ teaspoon pepper	*2 drops Tabasco sauce*
¾ teaspoon paprika	*6 tablespoons water*
6 tablespoons tomato ketchup	*8 frankfurters*

Chop the onion finely and cook in oil until it is soft and yellow. Add all the other ingredients except the frankfurters, and simmer together for 15 minutes. Split the frankfurters and put them into a thick frying pan. Pour over the sauce, and cook over low heat for 30 minutes, basting frequently while cooking.

BURGERS

Burgers made from beef, lamb, bacon, ham, pork or poultry

are easy to cook and eat. They can be served with salads or foil-cooked vegetables, and they make a handy snack in bread rolls. Whatever the type of burger, use the meat within 24 hours of purchase. A little fat is a good thing in minced meat which is to be cooked this way, as it will keep the meat moist and give it good flavour. Allow 1 lb minced beef for four average burgers, or six thin ones, and do not press the meat together too tightly. Shaped burgers may be stored in the freezer but will take a little longer to cook than fresh ones. The bread rolls to go with them can also be stored in the freezer. If the burgers have been wrapped in foil for freezing, they can be cooked on the grill without unwrapping. Burgers may be cooked on a well-greased metal sheet or in a thick frying pan over the grill, as they tend to break up when cooked on the grill alone.

For extra flavour, mix the meat with herbs, spices, seasoned salts, fresh or dried onion, fresh garlic or garlic powder. Dry soup mixes (onion or mushroom in particular) are also excellent for flavouring, and canned soups can be used as both seasoning and sauce. Those who like a 'hot' dish can add a pepper sauce such as Tabasco or Worcestershire to the meat before it is cooked.

Try serving the traditional burger made with beef with a wrapping of crisp bacon rashers; with a barbecue sauce; with a slice of cheese; with fried onions; with a sauce made from mushroom or tomato soup; or with piccalilli or chutney.

If you are cooking the burgers on a grill, spread them with a little softened butter. Grill over a very hot fire until brown and crisp. Brush the other side with butter and grill until done. Usually burgers need about 15 minutes' cooking time, and are best well-done unless the beef is very high quality, when it should be served rare.

IDEAL BEEFBURGERS

    1 lb freshly minced beef $\frac{1}{8}$ teaspoon pepper
    $\frac{1}{2}$ teaspoon salt

Mix the meat and seasonings very lightly. Shape into 4

patties. Grill for 3 to 5 minutes (but no more) on each side until they are just brown. The meat may be mixed with a little minced onion, or with a few spoonfuls of tomato juice or wine, or with a dash of Tabasco sauce. Some people like to bind the mixture with a small beaten egg.

FRIED BEEFBURGERS

1 lb freshly minced beef
½ teaspoon salt
⅛ teaspoon pepper
1 small minced onion

4 fl oz thin cream or
evaporated milk
Butter for frying

Mix together the beef, salt, pepper, onion, and cream very lightly, and shape the mixture into 4 patties. Cook in butter in a heavy frying pan over the barbecue grill, allowing 3 to 5 minutes each side until brown. These are good with a salad of sliced tomato and onion rings.

SURPRISE CHEESEBURGERS

1 lb freshly minced beef
½ teaspoon salt
⅛ teaspoon pepper
3 oz Cheddar cheese

1 dessertspoon Worcester-
shire sauce
1 dessertspoon mayonnaise
¼ teaspoon dry mustard

Mix the beef lightly with salt and pepper. Divide the meat into 8 pieces and shape into round patties. Mix the cheese with the sauce, mayonnaise and mustard, and put this mixture in the centre of half the meat patties. Top with the remaining patties and pinch the edges together carefully. Grill for 5 minutes each side over a hot fire.

BACON BURGERS

8-12 oz cooked bacon
4 oz fresh breadcrumbs
1 small chopped onion
Flour

Pepper
Pinch mixed herbs
1 large egg
4-6 streaky rashers

Mince bacon and onion, mix with breadcrumbs and seasoning, add sufficient beaten egg to bind mixture. Flour hands and form mixture into flat cakes, wrap each in a rasher of streaky bacon, then barbecue over a low fire. Cook slowly (if fire is very hot, place on a greased tin), about 15 minutes each side. Serve sandwiched in bread rolls with barbecue or tomato sauce.

LAMBURGERS

1 lb freshly minced lamb shoulder	*⅛ teaspoon ground allspice*
½ teaspoon salt	*4 tablespoons finely chopped parsley*
¼ teaspoon pepper	*4 rashers bacon*

Mix together the lamb and seasoning and shape into four rounds. Remove the rind from bacon rashers and flatten the rashers with the blade of a knife. Wrap a rasher around each lamburger. Grill over hot fire, turning once. Serve with tomato sauce.

FRIED LAMBURGERS

1 lb freshly minced lamb shoulder	*1 teaspoon Worcestershire sauce*
4 oz soft breadcrumbs	*1 oz butter*
1 tablespoon minced onion	*4 tablespoons redcurrant jelly*
½ teaspoon salt	
¼ teaspoon pepper	

Mix together the meat, breadcrumbs, onion and seasonings. Shape into six rounds. Heat butter in a thick frying pan and brown lamburgers on both sides. Drain off excess fat, and then add the redcurrant jelly to the pan. Cover and cook over a low heat for 15 minutes, turning once. These are good served with rings of pineapple heated through in the pan.

CHICKEN BURGERS

1 lb minced cooked chicken	*1 tablespoon bottled sauce*
1 small stick celery	*1 tablespoon chutney*
1 small onion	*Salt and pepper*
1 tablespoon mayonnaise	

Mince the chicken with the coarse blade, including a little

skin for extra flavour, and including the celery and onion. Mix with mayonnaise, sauce and chutney, and season to taste. Form into 6 rounds (they will be rather soft to handle) and grill on medium heat on both sides until golden. Handle very carefully, and put into soft rolls to serve.

BEEFBURGERS WITH BARBECUE SAUCE

1 lb freshly minced beef
1 small onion
Salt and pepper
8 fl oz tomato sauce

2 teaspoons Worcestershire sauce
4 drops Tabasco sauce

Mix together beef, chopped onion, salt and pepper. Form into four rounds. Mix together the sauces in a small saucepan and keep at the side of the fire. Grill the burgers over a hot fire, basting with the sauce while cooking for a total time of about 15 minutes. Serve in toasted buttered soft rolls with the remaining sauce.

HEARTY BURGERS

2 lb finely ground minced beef
8 tablespoons fresh breadcrumbs
½ teaspoon thyme

Salt and pepper
3 level teaspoons beef extract
1 egg

Mix the meat with breadcrumbs, thyme, salt and pepper, and beef extract. Add the beaten egg and mix well. Shape into ½ inch thick flat cakes and grill for 6 minutes on each side. Put hot burgers into split rolls or baps. Good with tomato slices, thinly-sliced raw onions, mustard, and crisp lettuce hearts.

FISH

Fish is delicious cooked on a barbecue, particularly when it is freshly caught. The fish can be whole or cut in steaks or fillets. Both cooked and raw shellfish can also be barbecued.

It is a good idea to cook in foil as this will keep it moist and prevent breakages, and give delicious juices.

Fish cooked on the grill will have a crisp brown skin, but must be carefully handled when turned or it will fall apart. Really firm-fleshed fish of a good size is best for straightforward grilling, and the grill rods should be well greased as fish tends to stick. A double sided grill with handles is best for fish as it can be turned easily. Fish can also be cooked in a heavy frying pan or on a hotplate over the grill. It is cooked when the flesh has turned opaque and flakes easily with a fork. Many fish have little natural fat, so it is a good idea to baste during cooking with butter or oil; a squeeze of lemon juice gives added flavour.

STUFFED FISH FILLETS

2 lb fish fillets	2 tablespoons chopped
8 oz soft white bread-	parsley
crumbs	Salt and pepper
4 tablespoons melted	
butter	

Use thin fish fillets for this recipe. Mix together breadcrumbs, butter, parsley, salt and pepper. Put a spoonful of the mixture on each fish fillet and roll it up. Fix with a small skewer. Brush the fish lightly with a little oil and cook on grill over medium heat for 15 minutes.

FISH FILLETS WITH PARSLEY BUTTER

2 lb fish fillets	2 oz butter
½ teaspoon salt	2 tablespoons chopped
Pepper	parsley
1 tablespoon salad oil	2 tablespoons lemon juice
1 tablespoon made mustard	

Mix the salt and pepper with the oil and brush this over the fish. Put on to a greased grill over medium heat and cook for 4 minutes each side until lightly browned. Mix together mustard, softened butter, parsley and lemon juice and spread half the mixture on the fish. Continue grilling for 5 minutes. Serve with remaining parsley butter.

RAINBOW TROUT IN FOIL

4 rainbow trout	*Fresh fennel, thyme or*
4 oz butter	*tarragon*
	Salt and pepper

Frozen trout may be used for this recipe. They should be thawed before cooking on the barbecue. Clean the fish and split down one side. Put 1 oz butter inside each fish, spreading it lightly. Put a branch of fennel, thyme or tarragon inside each fish, and season with salt and pepper. Brush 4 pieces of foil with oil and wrap each trout in a piece. Cook on the grill over a good heat, turning once, for about 30 minutes.

GRILLED SARDINES

12 fresh sardines	*1 tablespoon chopped*
2 tablespoons olive oil	*parsley*
1 tablespoon lemon juice	*2 oz butter*
	Salt and pepper

Before cooking the sardines, mix the lemon juice, parsley and seasoning with the butter. Form into a cylinder and chill in the refrigerator. Clean the fish and brush them with oil. Grill over a good heat on both sides. Serve with slices of parsley butter. Frozen sardines are often available and are suitable for cooking in this way.

GRILLED WHITING

4 whiting	*1 medium onion*
8 tablespoons olive oil	*Salt and pepper*
4 tablespoons chopped	
parsley	

Clean the whiting and slash the flesh diagonally on each side about three times. Mix together the oil, parsley and finely chopped onion. Put the whiting into this mixture and leave to stand for 1 hour. Grill over a good heat on both sides, basting with the oil and herb mixture during cooking.

GRILLED MACKEREL

4 mackerel	Salt and pepper
2 tablespoons salad oil	1 teaspoon caraway seeds
Juice of 1 lemon	

Clean the mackerel and slash the flesh diagonally on each side about three times. Brush with oil and lemon juice. Season with salt and pepper, and dust with caraway seeds. Grill on both sides over a good heat. Freshly caught mackerel is best.

GRILLED COD

4 cod steaks	¼ pint mayonnaise
Salt and pepper	1 tablespoon capers
Salad oil	

Brush the cod steaks with oil and season them well with salt and pepper. Grill on both sides over a good heat until golden. Stir the capers into the mayonnaise, and serve with the fish.

GRILLED SALMON

2 lb salmon steaks	1 tablespoon lemon juice
1 teaspoon fennel	Salt and pepper
4 tablespoons salad oil	

Mix together the fennel, oil and lemon juice, and leave to stand for 1 hour so that the herb is infused. Brush the salmon steaks with the oil and sprinkle on both sides with salt and pepper. Put on an oiled grill and cook for 8 minutes on each side over medium heat, basting occasionally with oil and lemon mixture.

BARBECUED CRAB

4 small cooked crabs	1 dessertspoon Worcester-
¾ pint chicken stock	shire sauce
1 tablespoon soy sauce	4 tablespoons bottled
1 tablespoon lemon juice	sauce
	½ teaspoon paprika

Prepare the body and leg meat of the crabs and return to the shells. Put into a baking tin. Simmer together the stock, soy sauce, lemon juice, Worcestershire sauce, bottled sauce and paprika. Pour over the crabs. Cook over a hot fire for 20 minutes, basting often. Put each crab on to a plate and cover with sauce.

BARBECUED LOBSTER

1-1½ lb lobsters   *Salt and pepper*
Butter or oil   *Lemon juice*

A lobster can be killed by inserting a knife into the back between the body and tail shells. Split lengthwise and clean. Wash and dry carefully, and try to open the lobsters as flat as possible. Brush with melted butter or oil, and sprinkle with salt and pepper. Grill over medium heat with shell side down for 15 minutes until shell browns. Turn over and brown the flesh for 5 minutes. Baste often with butter or oil. Serve with melted butter and lemon juice.

SKEWER COOKING

Cooking barbecue food on skewers is great fun, particularly for a small 'help yourself' kind of meal. It is not difficult to tackle, but needs a little planning. At least one skewer will be needed for each person, but it is a good idea to have a few spare ones. For first courses, or for fruit, short skewers about 5 inches long can be used, but for the main course, they need to be about 16 inches long. Turkey skewers can be used, but special barbecue skewers are available, sometimes with special handles and flame-protective guards to prevent scorched hands.

The food for skewers should be prepared in advance in the kitchen and marinaded if necessary, cut into the correct sized pieces. Arrange the food in bowls or on plates, so that each person can combine his own favourite foods, or you can prepare some skewers ready for cooking and leave some spare food for second helpings. Make sure the food is pressed close together on each skewer so that it does not slip off during cooking.

Cut most meat and fish into 1 or 1½ inch cubes. Marinade less tender cuts of meat for a few hours before cooking. Extra fat for lean cuts can be provided by a wrapping of thinly-sliced bacon, and this is very good with fish too. Alternatively, the skewered food can be brushed with oil or basting sauce before and during cooking. A sprinkling of herbs during cooking gives an aromatic flavouring, and a warm sauce is a tasty addition. Skewered food should be cooked over a hot fire and turned often. It is rather difficult to arrange the timing of different foods on the same skewer. In order that they should be cooked at the same time, cut the softer or fast-cooking foods into larger pieces, and the slow-cooking foods into smaller pieces. Use the firmest possible fruit and vegetables, and leave them unpeeled if they are tender. Here are some of the best foods for skewer-cooking; they can be cooked on their own, or mixed together:

MEAT. Leg or shoulder of lamb; steak; kidneys; liver; pork; bacon and ham; sausages; frankfurters; chicken livers.

FISH. Any firm-fleshed fresh or frozen fish; prawns; shrimps; crayfish; lobster; oysters; scallops.

VEGETABLES. Courgettes; peppers; small tomatoes; small onions; button mushrooms or mushroom caps; aubergines.

FRUIT. Apples; peaches; apricots; bananas; pineapple chunks; orange sections.

SHISHKEBAB

2 lb lean lamb	1 red pepper
16 rashers streaky bacon	Rosemary
2 onions	Salt and pepper
2 green peppers	Cooking oil

Cut the lamb into 1 inch cubes. Make the bacon rashers very thin with the flat blade of a knife. Roll lamb into pieces of bacon. Cut the onions and peppers into large pieces. Thread ingredients on skewers, alternating meat, onion and pepper pieces. Brush over lightly with oil and sprinkle with rosemary. Grill, turning the skewers frequently. Season with salt and pepper as soon as cooked.

FRENCH SKEWERED LAMB

2 lb lean lamb	*12 stoned olives*
2 green peppers	*24 button mushrooms*
8 bay leaves	*Paprika*
8 small tomatoes	*Cooking oil*
4 thick bacon rashers	

Cut the meat into cubes. Slice the peppers and cut the bacon into pieces. Arrange ingredients alternately on skewers. Brush lightly with oil and dust lightly with paprika. Grill, turning the skewers frequently.

SKEWERED LAMB CUTLETS

12 lamb cutlets	*Rosemary*
4 bacon rashers	*Bay leaves*
Made mustard	*Salt and pepper*
Chopped garlic	*Cooking oil*

Spread a little mustard lightly on the surface of the cutlets and sprinkle them with a little garlic and rosemary. Cut the bacon into pieces. Using 4 skewers, put cutlets on alternately with bacon and bay leaves. Brush lightly with oil. Grill, turning the skewers frequently. Season with salt and pepper as soon as cooked.

SKEWERED BEEF WITH COURGETTES

4 slices rump, sirloin or	*4 tomatoes*
fillet steak	*Olive oil*
2 courgettes	*Salt and pepper*

Cut the meat into squares. Cut the courgettes into rings and plunge them into boiling water for 1 minute. Drain well. Cut the tomatoes into quarters. Thread ingredients alternately on to skewers. Brush with oil and season with salt and pepper. Grill over high heat for 6 minutes.

SKEWERED VEAL

1 lb lean veal	*Salt and pepper*
8 tablespoons olive oil	*Thyme*
Juice of ½ lemon	*8 tomatoes*

Cut the meat into squares. Mix oil, lemon, salt and pepper, and thyme. Soak the meat in the marinade for 2 hours. Cut the tomatoes in quarters. Alternate meat and tomatoes on skewers. Grill and baste with a little of the marinade during cooking.

SKEWERED PORK WITH MUSTARD

8 oz lean pork	*Pepper*
4 oz bacon rashers	*Made mustard*
2 pork sausages	*Olive oil*

Cut the pork into small pieces. Cut the bacon rashers in half and form them into small rolls. Cut the sausages into rings. Thread ingredients alternately on the skewers. Season with pepper and brush with mustard lightly. Brush with oil and grill for about 10 minutes.

SKEWERED PORK WITH FRUIT

8 oz lean pork	*4 bay leaves*
4 oz bacon rashers	*Salt and pepper*
2 apples	*Olive oil*
2 oranges	

Cut the pork and bacon into pieces. Peel the apples and oranges and cut into quarters. Thread ingredients alternately on the skewers, together with bay leaves. Season with salt and pepper and brush with olive oil. Grill for about 10 minutes.

SKEWERED PORK WITH REDCURRANT JELLY

6 slices lean pork	*Oil*
1 lb chipolata sausages	*Redcurrant jelly*
6 oz streaky bacon rashers	*Salt and pepper*

Cut the pork into cubes. Twist the sausages into halves and

cut to form small sausages. Flatten the bacon rashers with the back of a knife, and form them into small rolls. Each rasher will make two bacon rolls. Thread pork, sausages and bacon rolls alternately on skewers. Brush with oil and melted red-currant jelly, and season with salt and pepper. Grill over high heat for 15 minutes, turning the skewers often.

SKEWERED MEATBALLS

1½ lb lean mince	*Salt and pepper*
2 eggs	*Breadcrumbs*
1 tablespoon chopped	*24 button mushrooms*
parsley	*8 small tomatoes*
Pinch of thyme	*Olive oil*

Mix the mince with 2 egg yolks and 1 egg white, parsley, thyme, salt and pepper. Shape into small balls and coat with the remaining egg white and breadcrumbs. Thread on skewers with mushrooms and tomatoes alternately. Brush with oil and grill, turning skewers frequently.

SKEWERED KIDNEYS

8 lambs' kidneys	*Thyme*
12 small onions	*Bay leaves*
8 streaky bacon rashers	*Salt and pepper*
8 small tomatoes	*Olive oil*
16 button mushrooms	

Remove skins and cores from kidneys and split in half. Season with salt and pepper. Put the kidney halves together and arrange on skewers with the onions, sliced bacon, tomatoes and mushrooms, and bay leaves. Brush with olive oil, season with salt and pepper, and grill.

SKEWERED LIVER AND BACON

8 oz calves' or lambs' liver	*Salt and pepper*
8 oz lean bacon	*Olive oil*

Cut the liver and bacon into 1 inch squares. Thread alternately on the skewers. Season with salt and pepper, and brush with oil. Grill over high heat for 5 minutes, turning the skewers frequently. This is even nicer if a few caraway seeds are sprinkled on during cooking.

SKEWERED HEARTS

8 oz lambs' heart	*Thyme*
4 tablespoons olive oil	*Salt and pepper*
1 tablespoon vinegar	

Cut the hearts into small cubes. Mix together oil, vinegar, thyme, salt and pepper. Leave the hearts in this marinade for 2 hours. Thread on skewers and grill over medium heat.

SEAFOOD SKEWERS

Marinade:

1 lemon	*Freshly ground black*
¼ pint olive oil	*pepper*
1 crushed garlic clove	1 bay leaf
¼ level teaspoon salt	

For the skewers:

5 rashers streaky bacon	8 large cooked prawns,
7½ oz packet frozen plaice	peeled
fillets thawed	1 large lemon, cut into 4
Salt and pepper	thick slices
3 (6-8 oz) crayfish tails,	
peeled	

Seafood sauce:

6 tablespoons thick mayon-	1 level teaspoon grated or
naise	finely chopped onions
1 tablespoon tomato purée	2 level teaspoons chopped
2 tablespoons lemon juice	parsley
1 tablespoon Worcester-	Salt and freshly ground
shire sauce	black pepper
1 level teaspoon grated	
lemon rind	

For the marinade, carefully pare rind from lemon with a

vegetable peeler or sharp knife. Squeeze juice from lemon and whisk together with oil, garlic, salt, pepper, bay leaf, and lemon rind.

Place bacon rashers on a board and stretch with the back of a round-bladed knife. Cut each rasher in half. Remove skin from plaice fillets and divide into 10 pieces. Place each piece on a rasher of bacon, season and roll up, enclosing the fish. Secure with a cocktail stick. Cut each crayfish tail into 4 equal pieces. Place bacon rolls and seafood in marinade and leave for 4 hours in a cool place, turning occasionally. Meanwhile prepare sauce by stirring all the ingredients together and seasoning to taste. Leave at least 4 hours before serving.

Remove seafood and strain marinade. Cut each lemon slice into 4 pieces. Remove cocktail sticks from bacon rolls and divide with seafood between 4 long or 8 shorter skewers, alternating with pieces of lemon. Place on barbecue for 8-10 minutes until fish is cooked, turning and brushing occasionally with marinade. Serve with seafood sauce. Other seafood such as scallops and lobster can be used as an alternative. If necessary, cut in appropriate sized pieces.

MUSSELS AND BACON

4 pints fresh mussels	*Fine breadcrumbs*
8 oz streaky bacon	*Cooking oil*
1 egg	*Salt and pepper*

The initial preparation of the mussels and the bacon is best done in the kitchen. Clean the mussels and put them into a heavy pan. Heat the pan until the mussels open. Remove them from the shells (saving the liquor for a soup if liked). Dip the mussels in beaten egg and toss in fine breadcrumbs. Flatten the bacon rashers with a flat-bladed knife until they are very thin, and cut them into strips. Form into bacon rolls. Arrange mussels and bacon rolls alternately on skewers. Brush with oil and season with salt and pepper. Cook over a hot grill, turning often. Serve with wedges of lemon, or tartare sauce.

SCALLOPS AND BACON

24 small scallops
8 oz thin streaky bacon
rashers

Cooking oil
Salt and pepper

Flatten the bacon rashers with a flat-bladed knife, and cut each rasher in half. Wrap a piece of bacon around each scallop and thread six on each skewer. Brush with oil and season with salt and pepper. Cook over a hot grill, turning often. Serve with wedges of lemon, or tartare sauce.

BACON SKEWERS

8 oz bacon rashers
4 oz stoned prunes
2 oranges

2 bananas
Olive oil

Make the bacon rashers very thin with the flat blade of a knife. Cut them into neat pieces. Soak the prunes overnight in water and drain. Peel oranges and break into sections, and cut bananas in chunks. Wrap each prune and piece of fruit in a piece of bacon. Alternate fruit pieces on skewers. Brush lightly with oil and grill until the bacon is crisp.

BACON AND KIDNEY KEBABS

9-12 rashers streaky bacon
6 kidneys

6 mushrooms
Olive oil or melted fat

Remove rind from bacon, cut each rasher in half and roll. Skin and halve kidneys, remove cores. Peel mushrooms, cut tomatoes in quarters. Thread ingredients on to skewers, brush with oil or fat, cook gently on cool part of barbecue, turning often, for 10-15 minutes. Serve on skewers with French bread and mustard.

SPICED BACON CURLS

Streaky bacon rashers
Chutney or mustard

Bananas

Remove rind from streaky rashers. Halve rashers and

spread with mustard or chutney. Wrap round pieces of banana, spear with cocktail sticks and grill. These can be garnished with pineapple.

SKEWERED FISH FINGERS

12 fish fingers	*24 button mushrooms*
8 thick bacon rashers	*6 tablespoons bottled sauce*

Cut the fish fingers into squares and leave until just thawed. Cut the bacon into squares. Thread alternate pieces of fish finger, bacon and button mushroom on to skewers. Brush with sauce and grill over a good heat, turning the skewers frequently. This is excellent for children's parties.

SPIT COOKING

Many barbecues are fitted with spits. While this cooking method requires some practice, the results are very worthwhile, particularly for a party. A motorised spit will need little attention once the meat or poultry is properly secured over a well-built fire. If a spit basket is available, it can be used for smaller cuts such as chops, steaks, chicken pieces and small whole fish.

PREPARING THE FOOD

A joint or poultry for roasting on a spit should be in as neat shape as possible. Meat should preferably be boned and tied, but it can be stuffed. Poultry should be carefully trussed, and it is important that there are no dangling wings or flaps of meat which may burn, and which can also unbalance the spit. Make sure that the meat or poultry is the correct weight for the spit so that it will rotate freely and not strain the motor.

For a boned joint, tie the meat at 1½ inch intervals, wrapping it in fat, salt pork or bacon before tying. If a joint is stuffed, it may need some metal skewers as well as string for tying. The meat should also be finished with a lengthwise tie connecting the crosswise strings to hold the ends of the meat firmly. A leg or shoulder joint is best cut in half to ensure balance on the spit. Rib or loin joints are also best cut in two or three sections.

Poultry which has been carefully trussed should also have one or two loops of string round the body to keep the legs and wings secure.

PUTTING FOOD ON THE SPIT

It is a good idea to put the meat or poultry in position and rotate it while the fire is cold, to see if it is evenly and correctly balanced. Try to judge where the bones are in the meat and where the area of greatest weight comes, so that the spit rod can be inserted where the weight will fall equally. Insert the spit rod through the centre of gravity and fix with spit forks. An imperfectly balanced spit will put the motor under strain and it will wear out quickly.

Poultry should be spitted parallel to the backbone, bringing the spit rod out between tail and legs; cook one bird in the centre of the spit. If small birds are being barbecued, dovetail them on the spit, alternating breast-side up and breast-side down, and push the birds together tightly. If very small birds are used, they can be spitted vertically, alternating heads and tails, and running the rod through the lower part of the breasts.

If a spit basket is used, be sure that all meat or fish is of the same thickness. Arrange the food closely together, alternating thick and thin pieces, or heads and tails. See that the food is flat, and make sure the cover is fastened securely to prevent food slipping to one side.

THE BARBECUE THERMOMETER

A meat thermometer will ensure perfectly cooked meat on the barbecue. A special barbecue thermometer, or an unpainted, all-metal meat thermometer can be used. It should be inserted in the meat before the spit rod is attached to the motor. Insert the tip of the thermometer into the thickest part of the meat, but do not let it touch the spit rod, or bone, or rest in fat. In large birds, the thickest part of the meat is between the breast and thigh. Put the thermometer at a slight angle to the spit rod so that it will not fall out as the spit revolves, and be sure that it does not touch the fire, drip pan or hood of the barbecue. The meat is cooked when the marked temperature is recorded on the thermometer.

THE DRIP PAN

The fire for spit-roasting should be at the back of the grill, with a drip pan at the front to catch the food juices. This prevents fat falling on the fire and causing flare-ups and smoke. Make a pan from heavy duty foil or use a shallow meat pan slightly longer than the meat which is being cooked. Put the pan a little forward but under the meat before starting to run the motor. Be sure that there are no coals or ashes under the drip pan which may cause the pan juices to burn.

The meat on the spit should be at a constant distance from the fire and just in front of it, so that heat is evenly maintained and all the juices run into the drip pan. Some herbs in the drip pan will flavour the pan juices for basting. As the food revolves on the spit, the juices which come to the surface will baste it. During cooking, the food can be basted with the pan juices, or with additional butter or oil, or with a barbecue sauce. Do not use a basting sauce until the last 10 minutes of spit cooking.

SPIT-ROASTED BEEF

2 lb topside beef	*Salt and pepper*
Sprig of rosemary	*Garlic butter (see method)*
Olive oil	

Put the beef on the spit, brush with oil and sprinkle with rosemary. When the meat is cooked, sprinkle with salt and pepper and serve with garlic butter. Make this by creaming butter with crushed garlic and chopped parsley to taste; form the butter into a cylinder and chill. Cut butter in circles to serve on slices of meat.

SPIT-ROASTED LAMB

3-4 lb leg or shoulder of
    lamb
8 cloves garlic
Salt and pepper

French mustard
Thyme
Olive oil

Split the garlic cloves into slivers, and insert them at regular
distances all over the meat with the aid of a sharp knife.
Season meat with salt and pepper. Brush over lightly with
mustard and oil and sprinkle thyme over the joint. Put on to
the spit and roast, basting with cooking juices.

SPIT-ROASTED STUFFED LAMB

4-5 lb boned leg or shoulder
    of lamb
8 oz bacon
1 medium onion
Salt and pepper

2 tablespoons redcurrant
    jelly
2 tablespoons fresh bread-
    crumbs

Mince the bacon and onion together and mix with the salt
and pepper, redcurrant jelly and breadcrumbs. Spread on
the lamb and roll up, securing tightly. Put on the spit and
baste occasionally with oil. Allow about 30 minutes per lb.

Another way of stuffing lamb is to lay kidneys along the
width of the joint, with a sprinkling of rosemary, salt and
pepper. Roll up tightly and secure very carefully as the
kidneys tend to slip out of the meat.

SPIT-ROASTED PORK

2 lb pork loin, boned and
    rolled
Olive oil
Thyme

Ground bay leaves
Sprigs of sage
Salt and pepper

Brush the meat with the oil and sprinkle with thyme and
bay leaves, salt and pepper. Put on sprigs of sage and roast
on spit until it is well-done.

SPIT-ROASTED CHICKEN

1 roasting chicken	*2 oz butter*
1 chicken liver	*Salt and pepper*
Sprig of rosemary	*Olive oil*

Stuff the chicken with the liver cut in small pieces, together with the rosemary and butter. Sprinkle well with salt and pepper and brush with olive oil. Put on to the spit and roast until golden, basting with the pan juices.

SPIT-ROASTED DUCK WITH ORANGE SAUCE

5 lb duck	*6 fl oz orange juice*
1 stick celery with leaves	*1 tablespoon lemon juice*
2 sprigs parsley	*2 oz soft brown sugar*
1 small onion	*Salt and pepper*
½ small orange	*Pinch of rosemary*
Salt and pepper	*Pinch of thyme*
Grated rind of 1 orange	

Truss the duck. Sprinkle salt and pepper inside, and fill with celery, parsley, onion cut in pieces and orange cut in pieces with the skin on. Put the duck on the spit and roast slowly, allowing about 2 hours. While the duck is cooking, mix together orange rind, orange and lemon juices, sugar, salt and pepper, and herbs and heat in a small saucepan to melt the sugar. Baste the duck with this sauce every 30 minutes. When the duck is cooked, skim off fat from the drip pan and pour the pan juices into a saucepan. Add the remaining barbecue sauce, and simmer until slightly thickened. Serve with the duck and with a few peeled orange sections.

COOKING IN FOIL

Foil is marvellous cooking equipment for the barbecue. Meat, poultry, fish and vegetables cooked in foil have a delicious flavour, are moist and juicy, and retain their food values. Portions can be cooked individually or for a large party; it is generally easier to deal with small foil packets which can be moved around on the grill or in the fire as space is needed.

Food can be prepared and wrapped beforehand, and kept cool in the kitchen or refrigerator. A generous piece of foil is needed for each package and must not be punctured. All folds must be carefully finished off to avoid seepage of juices. It is best to brush the inside of the foil with a light coating of oil or melted butter before putting in the ingredients. These should be seasoned before cooking. If guests are late, the foil packages can be kept warm at the side of the fire without drying out. To serve, either put the packages on paper plates and let each person open his own, or open the packages yourself and tuck in a little parsley or watercress for colour.

To wrap food neatly in foil, you must use enough to cover the food and make adequate folds. Use a single thickness of heavy-duty foil, or a double thickness of ordinary foil. Put the food just off-centre of the foil. Bring up the foil over the food so that the edges meet on the three open sides. Make folds at least ½-inch deep, folding over two or three times to make a firm package, leaving plenty of air space around the food. Small parcels of food can be finished by drawing up the foil in a bunch and finishing it in a twist on top of the food, but this is only suitable for parcels which do not have to be turned frequently.

Food wrapped in foil can be placed in a low heat directly in the fire; it can also be put on a grill or hotplate over a hot fire.

In this section there are recipes for cooking meat, poultry and fish in foil. Ideas for preparing other foods will be found in 'Vegetables and Salads', 'Bread', and 'Finishing the Meal'.

PORK CHOPS IN FOIL WITH COURGETTES

1 pork chop per person

For each pork chop:

1 courgette	*1 dessertspoon brown sugar*
1 tablespoon butter	*Salt and pepper*

Put the pork chop in the centre of a piece of foil. Add the

courgette cut in $\frac{1}{2}$ inch rings. Dot with butter and sprinkle with sugar. Season well with salt and pepper. Form the foil into a parcel and cook over hot fire for 1 hour, turning often.

VEAL CHOPS IN FOIL

4 veal chops	*Salt and pepper*
1 fl oz olive oil	*1 tablespoon tomato paste*
4 cloves garlic	*1 teaspoon basil*

Brush the chops on both sides with the oil and grill for 2 minutes on each side. Put each chop on to a square of foil and scatter with chopped garlic. Add a dab of tomato paste, and season with salt, pepper and basil. Form the foil into a parcel and grill for 10 minutes on each side over medium heat.

VEAL CHOPS WITH MUSHROOM STUFFING

4 veal chops	*2 oz chopped parsley*
3 oz bacon rashers	*Salt and pepper*
4 oz button mushrooms	*1 fl oz olive oil*
1 medium onion	

Cut the bacon into small squares and put into a saucepan. Heat gently until the fat runs, then add the chopped mushrooms and onions and cook gently until soft. Add a little of the olive oil, if necessary, to prevent burning. Mix with the parsley and season to taste with salt and pepper (be careful with the salt if the bacon is already salty). Make a slit in each chop and put in the stuffing. Brush the chops on both sides with the olive oil and wrap each in foil. Put on the grill and cook over medium heat for 15 minutes each side.

CHICKEN IN FOIL

3 lb chicken	*4 tablespoons chopped*
1 lb sausage meat	*mixed herbs*
3 oz white breadcrumbs	*1 egg yolk*
Water or stock	*Salt and pepper*
	Salad oil

Mix the sausage meat, the breadcrumbs soaked in water or

stock, herbs, egg yolk, and seasoning. Stuff the chicken with this mixture. Brush a sheet of foil with oil and wrap the chicken firmly. Put the parcel into hot charcoal and let it cook for 45 minutes, turning once.

CHICKEN AND VEGETABLES IN FOIL
1 chicken joint per person
For each chicken joint:

1 potato	*Salt and pepper*
1 tomato	*Few drops Worcestershire*
1 medium onion	*sauce*
2 mushrooms	*1 oz butter*
2 rings green pepper	

Put the chicken joint in the centre of a piece of foil. Add vegetables cut in medium slices. Season well with salt, pepper and Worcestershire sauce. Dot with butter and fold the foil into a packet. Cook on grill over hot fire for 40 minutes, turning the packet often.

HAM IN FOIL
1-inch thick slice cooked ham per person
For each ham slice:

1 tablespoon brown sugar	*1 pineapple slice*
½ teaspoon mixed mustard	*½ oz butter*
1 clove	

1 tablespoon orange marmalade per ham slice may be substituted for the brown sugar and mustard. Put each ham slice on to a piece of foil. Brush with sugar and mustard, or with marmalade, and top with the pineapple slice which can be fresh or canned. Stick the clove into the pineapple. Form the foil into a parcel, and dot with butter. Cook on grill over a hot fire, turning once, for 30 minutes. Good with a green salad and jacket potatoes.

BLACK PUDDINGS IN FOIL

3 black puddings	*3 tablespoons lemon juice*
2 teaspoons dry mustard	*3 oz fresh breadcrumbs*

Pierce the black puddings twice with a fork. Make up

mustard with lemon juice and spread over the puddings. Roll
them in breadcrumbs. Brush some foil with oil and put each
black pudding in a separate piece. Grill over high heat for
15 minutes, turning often.

FISH IN FOIL
   Butter   *Salt and pepper*
   1 medium onion   *Fresh herbs*
   Whole fish (1-3 lb)

Use a large piece of heavy duty foil which will enclose the
whole fish. Spread some butter on the centre. Slice the onion
thinly and put a few slices on the butter. Clean the fish and
remove the head and tail. Sprinkle salt and pepper inside the
fish, put it on top of the onion slices and cover with the remaining onion and some herbs. Use tarragon, parsley, fennel,
dill or thyme as you choose. Sprinkle with salt and pepper and
dot with a little butter. Make foil into a parcel, ensuring that
all folds are secure. Cook on grill over medium heat, allow 15
minutes (1 lb fish), 25 minutes (2 lb fish) or 35 minutes (3 lb
fish). Turn the parcel two or three times during cooking. To
serve, open foil and bend back edges. Serve fish from the
bones, spooning over the juices which are held in the foil.

PRAWNS IN FOIL
   1 lb shelled prawns   ¼ *teaspoon basil*
   1 clove garlic   *3 tablespoons lemon juice*
   4 oz melted butter   *Salt and pepper*
   ¼ *teaspoon rosemary*

Prawns or scampi can be used fresh or frozen; frozen ones
should be thawed until they are separate. Crush the garlic
and stir into the butter with the herbs. Heat gently in a heavy
saucepan for a few minutes. Remove from heat and add the
lemon juice. Use a piece of foil for each person, and divide
prawns into portions (about 6 prawns for a first course; 12-15
for a main course). Pour on the butter mixture and season
with salt and freshly ground pepper. Make foil into parcels

and grill over medium heat for 10 minutes. Serve with plenty of crusty bread.

SAUCES, MARINADES, SAVOURY BUTTERS AND SALAD DRESSINGS

Barbecue food needs the complementary flavouring of sauces, which add both colour and zest to all kinds of meat and fish. Spicy tomato-based sauces and sweet-sour mixtures are popular; some of these are used for basting food during cooking, adding moisture, flavour and a deliciously glazed appearance. Other sauces, relishes and butters are used at the time of serving.

Sauces are best cooked in heavy-based saucepans at the side of the grill. If necessary, they can be pre-cooked in the kitchen. A wooden spoon should be used for stirring, and the sauce can be basted over the meat with a small paint brush, or with a bundle of herbs which will give extra flavour. Sauces which are to be used for long-cooking should contain oil. Those which contain tomato are best brushed on the food during the last ten minutes' cooking time, but others can be used for basting as soon as cooking begins.

If a sauce is not to be used, savoury butters give meat and poultry a delicate flavour. The *flavoured butters* should be made well in advance and shaped into cylinders, wrapped in foil and refrigerated; they can then be sliced in neat circles and put on to meat, fish or poultry just before serving.

Marinades not only give extra flavour, but help to tenderise meat and poultry. If possible, let a marinade mellow at room temperature for 24 hours before adding to meat. If marinades are intended to tenderise, they should contain vinegar, wine or lemon juice, and it is best to keep them in glass or china containers. When they are kept in a refrigerator, they should be covered to prevent the smell spreading to other foods. Most meat only needs to be marinated for a few hours at room temperature, but can be left overnight. The marinade can be used as a basting sauce during cooking, or can be heated and served with the food.

If a salad or vegetables are served with a spicily-sauced meat, the *salad dressing* or vegetable topping should be kept simple. If the basic main course is simple, then a more exotic dressing for the salad or vegetables is suitable.

UNCOOKED BARBECUE SAUCE

2 tablespoons ketchup	½ teaspoon mustard
1 tablespoon vinegar	1 tablespoon lemon juice
1 dessertspoon Worcester-	1 tablespoon brown sugar
shire sauce	

Mix all ingredients well together.

COOKED BARBECUE SAUCE

2 tablespoons butter	2 tablespoons made
1 chopped onion	mustard
1 chopped red or green	3 tablespoons ketchup
pepper	1 tablespoon Worcester-
2 tablespoons brown sugar	shire sauce
Salt and pepper	1 tablespoon lemon juice

Simmer all ingredients for 15 minutes. If too thin, add a little cornflour (1 heaped tablespoon mixed to a smooth paste with vinegar).

CURRY BASTING SAUCE

3 oz butter	½ teaspoon salt
2 oz plain flour	Shake of pepper
1 dessertspoon curry	1 pint chicken or beef stock
powder	

Melt the butter and take off the fire. Stir in the flour, curry powder, salt and pepper until smooth. Stir in the stock and heat over low fire until the sauce is thickened. Use to baste chicken or lamb and to serve with the food.

INDONESIAN SAUCE

1 tablespoon salad oil
4 level tablespoons peanut
  butter
¼ pint tomato ketchup
3 tablespoons Worcester-
  shire sauce
Pinch garlic powder to
  taste
¼ level teaspoon salt

Heat oil gently in pan and add peanut butter. Continue heating gently, stirring occasionally, until peanut butter begins to thicken and darkens slightly. Remove from heat immediately and stir in tomato ketchup and Worcestershire sauce. Season to taste with garlic powder and salt. Leave for 2 hours before using. Reheat gently. Serve with barbecued chicken and steaks. This can also be used as a baste for chicken. Add a little water if sauce is too thick.

GOLDEN BARBECUE SAUCE

2 oz butter or margarine
1 tablespoon chopped green
  pepper (optional)
1 tablespoon chopped
  onion
2 tablespoons mild mustard
1 tablespoon brown sugar
¼ pint beef stock
¼ teaspoon salt
Shake of pepper
Dash of Cayenne pepper

Melt butter. Add green pepper and onion and cook over low heat until soft and lightly browned. Blend in mustard and sugar. Stir in stock and seasonings. Simmer gently about 5 minutes. If green pepper is not used 1 tablespoon parsley can be added. Spoon over burgers or meat several times during grilling.

SHERRY BASTING SAUCE

4 fl oz sherry
4 fl oz salad oil
1 teaspoon minced onion
1 teaspoon brown sugar
½ teaspoon made mustard
Pinch of thyme
½ teaspoon marjoram
½ teaspoon salt
¼ teaspoon pepper

Mix all ingredients together, and stir or shake vigorously. Use for steak, lamb or chicken.

SWEET AND SOUR BASTING SAUCE

1 tablespoon cooking oil	*4 fl oz pineapple juice*
½ teaspoon salt	*3 oz brown sugar*
½ green pepper	*4 fl oz wine vinegar*
1 clove garlic	*1 teaspoon soy sauce*

Put the oil into a saucepan. Add the salt, finely chopped green pepper and whole garlic clove. Simmer for 5 minutes. Take out the garlic. Add the pineapple juice, sugar, vinegar and soy sauce and simmer for 5 minutes. Use for pork or chicken.

QUICK BASTING SAUCE

1 tablespoon cooking oil	*4 fl oz vinegar*
1 small onion	*2 oz brown sugar*
1 clove garlic	*6 oz concentrated tomato*
½ teaspoon mustard	*paste*
1 dessertspoon Worcester-	*4 fl oz water*
shire sauce	

Put the oil in a saucepan with the minced onion and garlic. Simmer for 5 minutes. Add all the other ingredients and simmer for 10 minutes, stirring well, before using.

LAMB MARINADE

8 fl oz olive oil	*4 tablespoons chopped*
Juice of 1 lemon	*parsley*
2 cloves garlic	*Sprig of thyme*
1 onion	*Salt and pepper*

Put the oil into a bowl with the lemon juice. Chop the garlic and onion finely, and add to the oil. Stir in the parsley and add the thyme, salt and pepper. Leave the meat in this marinade for 2 or 3 hours.

POULTRY MARINADE

2 carrots	Salt and pepper
2 onions	Thyme, parsley and bay-leaf
2 cloves garlic	
4 tablespoons olive oil	8 fl oz white wine

Cut the carrots and onions into thin slices, and chop the garlic. Cook in oil until lightly browned. Add salt and pepper and herbs, and just cover with water. Simmer for 10 minutes. Add the wine, bring to the boil, and then cool before using.

MARINADE FOR PORK

2 oz sugar	2 fl oz soy sauce
½ teaspoon ground ginger	2 fl oz salad oil
½ teaspoon mustard	2 cloves crushed garlic
½ teaspoon salt	2 fl oz water
1 tablespoon black treacle	

Mix together sugar, ginger, mustard, salt, treacle, soy sauce, and salad oil. Add crushed garlic and water and stir or shake vigorously before using.

RED MEAT MARINADE

4 fl oz dry white wine	Thyme, parsley and bay-leaf
4 fl oz wine vinegar	
4 fl oz olive oil	2 cloves garlic
1 small onion	4 whole cloves
1 small carrot	Salt and pepper

Mix together the wine, vinegar and oil. Cut the onion and carrot into thin slices, and chop the garlic. Mix into the wine and add the cloves, salt and pepper.

WHITE MEAT MARINADE

4 fl oz wine vinegar	Good sprig of marjoram
8 fl oz dry white wine	Salt and pepper
2 onions	

Mix the vinegar and wine and add the onions cut in thin slices. Add the marjoram, salt and pepper.

HERB MARINADE FOR LAMB OR CHICKEN

4 fl oz olive or salad oil
2 fl oz lemon juice
½ teaspoon salt
¼ teaspoon pepper
½ teaspoon marjoram

½ teaspoon thyme
2 tablespoons parsley
1 clove garlic
1 large onion

Mix together oil, lemon juice, salt and pepper. Chop the herbs finely, and chop the garlic and onion. Mix all ingredients together and use for lamb or chicken.

ROSEMARY MARINADE FOR LAMB OR CHICKEN

2 fl oz olive or salad oil
2 fl oz wine vinegar
½ teaspoon salt

¼ teaspoon pepper
1 teaspoon rosemary
1 medium onion

Mix together oil, vinegar, salt and pepper, and rosemary. Add finely sliced onion. Use for lamb or chicken. Rosemary has a very strong and distinctive flavour, but goes beautifully with these two meats. Try it out on the family first if you think that guests might be a little uncertain about the flavour.

SOUR CREAM MARINADE FOR CHICKEN

8 fl oz commercial sour
    cream
1 dessertspoon lemon juice
2 cloves garlic
¼ teaspoon white pepper

¼ teaspoon salt
¼ teaspoon paprika
¼ teaspoon celery salt
½ teaspoon Worcestershire
    sauce

Mix together the sour cream and lemon juice. Crush the garlic and add to the cream with all the other ingredients. Put chicken joints into a bowl and cover with the marinade. Chill in a refrigerator overnight before cooking.

GARLIC BUTTER

4 oz butter	*1 clove garlic*

Soften the butter, but do not melt it. Crush the garlic and work it into the butter. Form into a cylinder, wrap in foil or greaseproof paper and chill. Cut in rings to serve with steak.

MUSTARD BUTTER

4 oz butter	*5 drops Worcestershire*
1 teaspoon made mustard	*sauce*

Soften the butter, but do not melt it. Stir in the mustard and Worcestershire sauce. Form into a cylinder, wrap in foil or greaseproof paper and chill. Cut in rings to serve with steak, pork or poultry.

PARSLEY BUTTER

4 oz butter	*1 tablespoon finely*
1 tablespoon lemon juice	*chopped parsley*

Soften the butter, but do not melt it. Stir in the lemon juice and parsley. Form into a cylinder, wrap in foil or greaseproof paper and chill. Cut in rings to serve with steak, chops, poultry or fish.

LOW CALORIE DRESSING

4 tablespoons tomato juice (or half orange and half lemon or grapefruit juice)	*1 teaspoon made mustard*
	Sprinkling of pepper and salt
½ teaspoon finely chopped onion	

Blend ingredients. Further flavouring may be added, such as 1 tablespoon chopped parsley or mint or green pepper. Use with green or vegetable salads.

BLUE CHEESE DRESSING

4 oz cottage cheese
2 oz blue cheese, crumbled
3 tablespoons salad cream

2 tablespoons single cream
or top of milk
1 teaspoon made mustard
1 dessertspoon lemon juice

Blend ingredients smoothly. Serve chilled, topped with a dusting of paprika or finely chopped parsley or chives. Use on crisp lettuce hearts.

TANGY DRESSING

2 tablespoons honey
2 egg yolks
2 tablespoons lemon juice
1 tablespoon French
mustard or 1 teaspoon
made mustard

½ teaspoon grated lemon
rind
3 tablespoons salad oil

Beat together all ingredients except oil. Beat in oil very gradually until thick. Store in cold place. Whisk before using. Use sparingly for salad fruits and lettuce hearts.

YOGURT SALAD DRESSING

¼ pint plain yogurt
1 teaspoon each of chopped
parsley, chives or onion

Made mustard

Blend ingredients and season further to taste. Celery or garlic salt is good with this. Chopped cucumber also blends well and it is delicious with salads and fish.

NIPPY SAUCE

2 tablespoons salad cream
(not mayonnaise)

1 teaspoon made mustard
1 tablespoon lemon juice

Blend ingredients well. Use as a dressing for cold green peas or beans.

DEVILLED CHEESE CREAM

5 oz carton soured cream	*6 oz grated Cheddar cheese*
2 tablespoons HP sauce	*1 teaspoon lemon juice*
2 finely chopped spring onions	*Salt and pepper*

Blend soured cream and sauce. Fold in remaining ingredients. Serves 4-6 as a topping for 4-6 large jacket potatoes or is sufficient dressing for 1½ lb cold, cooked, sliced potatoes.

SIMPLE HOT SAUCE

2 large onions	*Pinch of ground ginger*
6 oz tomato purée	*Salt*
1 tablespoon paprika	*1 pint chicken stock*

Chop the onions finely and soften in a little oil. Add the tomato purée, paprika, ginger, and salt to taste, and blend smoothly with stock. Cook over low heat for 15 minutes. This is very good with chicken or sausages.

SPICY SALAD DRESSING

3 tablespoons oil	*1 tablespoon HP sauce*
1 tablespoon lemon juice	

Whisk together all ingredients until blended. Serve with sliced tomatoes, cucumber, beetroot, green peppers.

DEVILLED DRESSING

1 tablespoon finely grated horseradish	*1 tablespoon made mustard*
2 tablespoons redcurrant jelly	*Juice of a large orange and finely peeled twist of rind*

Mix ingredients and simmer 3 minutes. Remove orange peel. Serve cold, whisking well before serving. Good with ham or pork.

MUSTARD HOLLANDAISE

1 egg yolk	*1 tablespoon tomato purée*
1 tablespoon caster sugar	*1 oz butter*
1 tablespoon French	*3 tablespoons vinegar*
mustard	

Blend ingredients. Cook over low heat (best over boiling water) for 2 minutes, stirring constantly. Use with fish, veal or pork.

SOURED CREAM SAUCE

2 egg yolks	*1 teaspoon made mustard*
¼ pint soured cream (if not	*1 dessertspoon finely*
available, sour fresh	*chopped parsley*
cream with 1 dessert-	*Pepper and salt to taste*
spoon lemon juice)	

Beat egg yolks, blend in cream and cook over boiling water until thick and smooth. Stir in mustard and parsley and season with pepper and salt. Use for chicken, fish or vegetables.

MUSTARD TOPPER

¼ pint cultured sour cream	*1 dessertspoon finely*
(or fresh cream and 1	*minced onion*
dessertspoon lemon juice,	*½ level teaspoon salt*
or use salad cream)	*Dash of white pepper and*
2 tablespoons mild mustard	*cayenne*

Blend ingredients. Use cold or heat over boiling water. Serve with hot frankfurters, grilled fish or gammon.

CUCUMBER SAUCE

3 tablespoons mayonnaise	*½ teaspoon minced onion*
4 tablespoons chopped	*1 dessertspoon mild*
cucumber	*mustard*

Mix the ingredients and season further to taste with pepper, salt and paprika. Good with ham or fish.

SWEET AND SOUR SAUCE

8 oz can pineapple slices
1 grated carrot
1 grated small onion
*1 inch length of cucumber,
cut into ¼ inch cubes*
1 tablespoon vinegar

*2 tablespoons Worcester-
shire sauce*
Salt and pepper
2 level teaspoons cornflour
1 tablespoon water

Drain pineapple and make juice up to ½ pint with water. Chop pineapple and place in a pan with carrot, onion and cucumber. Add vinegar, pineapple juice and Worcestershire sauce and bring to the boil. Simmer gently for 5 minutes. Season. Mix cornflour with water, blend into sauce and bring to the boil, stirring. Serve hot with gammon and bacon joints, hamburgers and sausages.

SPECIAL BARBECUE SAUCE

2 oz butter
1 finely chopped onion
1 clove crushed garlic
2 tablespoons vinegar
*¼ pint + 5 tablespoons
water*
*1 level tablespoon made
English mustard*
*2 level tablespoons
demerara sugar*

*1 thick slice lemon, pips
removed*
⅛ teaspoon cayenne pepper
*2 tablespoons Worcester-
shire sauce*
*6 tablespoons tomato
ketchup*
2 tablespoons tomato purée
Salt and pepper

Melt butter in pan and fry onion and garlic gently for 3 minutes. Stir in vinegar, water, mustard, sugar, lemon and cayenne pepper. Bring to boil and simmer for 15 minutes. Stir in remaining ingredients, season to taste and continue for a further 5 minutes. Remove lemon and serve.

RICH MUSHROOM SAUCE

½ oz butter
1 finely chopped onion
6 oz chopped mushrooms
¼ pint red wine
¼ pint beef stock

2 level teaspoons cornflour
1 tablespoon Worcestershire sauce
Salt and pepper

Melt butter in a pan and fry onion gently for 3 minutes. Add mushrooms and fry for a further 2 minutes. Add wine and beef stock and bring to the boil. Turn down heat and simmer for 10 minutes. Blend cornflour with Worcestershire sauce and pour on a little of the hot sauce, stirring. Return to pan and bring to boil, stirring. Simmer gently for 2 minutes, season to taste and serve with barbecued poultry, meat or fish.

QUICK CHUTNEY

3 tablespoons HP sauce
1 tablespoon tomato purée
5 oz apple purée
2 dessert apples, peeled, cored and roughly chopped

1 banana, peeled and roughly chopped
2 oz raisins
½ oz chopped almonds
½ oz chopped walnuts

Blend together sauce, tomato purée and apple purée. Add remaining ingredients and mix well. This will keep covered in a refrigerator for up to 2 weeks.

HOT DEVILLED CREAM SAUCE

4 tablespoons single cream   1 tablespoon HP sauce

Mix ingredients together in a pan and heat gently until hot. Do not boil. Serve with fish or chicken.

ZESTY HORSERADISH SAUCE

¼ pint double cream
1 tablespoon lemon juice
1 teaspoon horseradish sauce

2 teaspoons Worcestershire sauce
2 spring onions, finely chopped

Mix together double cream and lemon juice. Blend in

remaining ingredients. Allow to stand for at least 4 hours before serving. Serve with barbecued steaks and hamburgers or use as a topping for jacket potatoes.

SWEETCORN RELISH

7 oz can sweetcorn kernels	*1 small chopped green*
5 oz apple purée	*pepper*
2 tablespoons HP sauce	*1 small finely chopped*
2 chopped sticks celery	*onion*
1 chopped red pepper	*¼ level teaspoon salt*

Mix together all ingredients. Allow to stand for at least 4 hours before serving. Serve with barbecued chicken, hamburgers or sausages or with jacket potatoes.

VEGETABLES AND SALADS

A simple salad is a good accompaniment to grilled meat, poultry or fish. Those made from only one or two vegetable components are more attractive than mixed bowls of all the salad ingredients. A selection of a green salad, a starch salad containing rice or potatoes, and a refreshing salad of tomatoes, beans or cucumber, will give guests plenty of choice.

Vegetables need not be neglected at the barbecue, and can be rather unusual. Potatoes in their jackets are always popular, and can be cooked in the ashes or on the grill, and in various ways wrapped in foil. Foil is useful for cooking many kinds of vegetables and the packets can be cooked on the grill, or in the ashes if there is little room to spare. Some vegetables, such as baked beans, can be kept hot in heavy casseroles at the side of the fire, or in heavy saucepans on the grill. If time or space is short, such vegetables can be partly prepared in the kitchen and brought out to the barbecue for finishing.

BAKED POTATOES
Potatoes   *Butter or bacon fat*

Scrub the potatoes and dry them. Rub with a little butter

or bacon fat and wrap in foil. Put on grill over medium fire and cook for 50 minutes. They may be placed round the outer edge of the grill but will take slightly longer to cook. They can also be cooked in the fire if space on the grill is limited. Pierce with a fork to see if potatoes are done, or squeeze with the fingers (wear gloves for this). To serve, open the foil and cut a cross on top of each potato. Squeeze slightly and dot with butter. They could be served with sour cream and chives, cottage cheese, or crumbled cooked bacon.

POTATOES IN FOIL

8 medium potatoes
¼ pint fresh or soured
  cream

4 tablespoons chopped
  mixed herbs
Salt and pepper

Wash the potatoes but do not peel them. Cook for 10 minutes in boiling water. Dry them on kitchen paper and prick the skins well with a fork. Wrap each one in foil and cook on the grill over a good heat for 15 minutes. To serve, open the foil, cut the potatoes in half, and cover with cream, herbs, and seasoning to taste.

FOILED POTATO CHIPS

Potato chips (fresh or
  frozen)
Onion

Salt and pepper
Butter

Cut potatoes into chips, or use frozen ones. Put each portion into heavy-duty foil. Sprinkle with a little very finely chopped onion, salt and pepper, and flakes of butter. Fold the foil into packages and cook over medium fire. Cook 40 minutes for fresh potatoes, or 25 minutes for frozen ones.

FOILED POTATOES AND ONIONS

4 large potatoes
2 oz butter

2 medium onions
Salt and pepper

Peel the potatoes and cut each one crosswise in four slices. Butter between the slices and on top. Cut onions in rings, and put rings between potato slices. Season with salt and pepper. Wrap each potato in heavy-duty foil and put into the coals of the fire. Bake for 45 minutes. Sprinkle with some chopped parsley and serve.

FOILED CORN
Corn on the cob   Salt and pepper
Butter

The husks of the corn can be left on, but the 'silk' should be removed. Brush the cobs with melted butter and season with salt and pepper. Cover with the husks and wrap in foil. Use two layers of foil if the fire is very hot, or if the corn is to be cooked in the fire itself. Cook for 25 minutes, turning 2 or 3 times. If frozen corn is used, it should be defrosted first.

FOILED ONIONS
Large onions   Salt and pepper
Butter

Wash the onions, but leave the skins on. Wrap each one in a square of heavy-duty foil. Cook on grill over medium heat for 50 minutes, turning occasionally. The onions will be done when they are soft to the touch. Open the foil and push back the onion skins. Add butter, salt and pepper.

FOILED SUMMER VEGETABLES
Courgettes   Garlic
Tomatoes   Mixed fresh herbs
Onions   Butter
Salt and pepper

Slice the courgettes and onions thinly. Peel the tomatoes and cut them in quarters. Mix vegetables and put each portion on to a square of heavy-duty foil. Season with salt and pepper, a little chopped garlic and a sprinkling of herbs. Dot with butter and make foil into packages. Grill over medium heat for 30 minutes, turning once.

FOILED FROZEN VEGETABLES

1 packet frozen vegetables
(peas, sweetcorn kernels
or mixed vegetables)

4 tablespoons water
Salt and pepper
1 oz butter

Leave the vegetables until partly defrosted. Put into the centre of a piece of foil. Add water, seasoning and butter. Fold foil into a parcel. Cook at the edge of the fire for 25 minutes, shaking the parcel occasionally. This is very useful for an impromptu barbecue if fresh vegetables or salads are not easily obtainable.

STUFFED TOMATOES

8 medium tomatoes
4 tablespoons chopped
parsley
1 medium onion

3 oz white breadcrumbs
Salt and pepper
Salad oil

Cut the tomatoes in half and scoop out the seeds. Brush the insides of the tomatoes with oil. Chop the parsley and onion very finely and mix together with the breadcrumbs, salt and pepper. Put the mix into hollow tomatoes and grill over a low heat. These are very good with lamb chops and with sausages.

GRILLED MUSHROOMS

24 large mushrooms
Salad oil
4 cloves garlic
1 medium onion

4 tablespoons chopped
parsley
Salt and pepper

Use large mushrooms with open caps, and remove the stalks. Brush with oil and grill over a low heat. Meanwhile, chop the garlic, onion and parsley very finely. When the mushrooms are nearly cooked, season them with salt and pepper, and put a spoonful of onion and herb mixture in the centre of each.

FRIED ONION RINGS

3 large onions	*½ teaspoon salt*
4 oz plain flour	*1 egg*
¼ teaspoon baking powder	*8 fl oz milk*

Cut the onions into ¼ inch slices and separate them into rings. Mix together the egg and milk and soak the onion rings in this. Drain the onion rings. Work the flour, baking powder and salt into the liquid to make a batter. Dip the onion rings into this batter and fry in small batches in deep hot fat or oil. Keep them separated with a fork during frying. Cook until golden brown and drain on kitchen paper. Serve very hot with steak. If you do not want to cook with deep fat on the barbecue, cook the onion rings in the kitchen, and reheat them in shallow fat just before serving.

GRILLED AUBERGINES

4 large aubergines	*2 teaspoons marjoram*
Salt	*Olive oil*
Pepper	

Do not peel the aubergines, but cut them across into ½ inch slices. Sprinkle salt on both sides of the slices and put into a colander for 1 hour, so that the salt draws out the juices. Rinse in cold water and dry on kitchen paper. Sprinkle slices with pepper and marjoram after brushing with oil. Grill over a hot fire for 5 minutes, turning once, until the aubergines are soft and slightly browned.

BARBECUED BEANS

4 oz streaky bacon	*16 oz can baked beans*
1 oz butter	*1 tablespoon horseradish*
2 sticks celery	*sauce*
1 medium onion	*1 teaspoon French mustard*

Cut the bacon into small pieces and put into a heavy pan. Heat gently until the fat starts to run. Add the butter and the finely chopped celery and onion. Cook gently until golden.

Add the beans, horseradish sauce and mustard. Cover and place over a medium heat until the beans are hot. Serve with sausages. This dish can be started in the kitchen, and then the beans can be transferred to the barbecue grill when needed.

MIXED GREEN SALAD

1 large lettuce	*2 teaspoons mixed fresh*
1 cucumber	*herbs*
4 spring onions	*Salad oil*
1 green pepper	*Vinegar*
	Salt and pepper

Wash the lettuce, drain and chill. Tear into pieces and put into a bowl. Mix with thinly sliced cucumber, thinly sliced spring onions, chopped green pepper, and fresh herbs. Mix a dressing, allowing three parts oil to one part vinegar with salt and pepper. Pour over the salad just before serving and toss lightly.

RATATOUILLE

2 onions	*4 large tomatoes*
2 aubergines	*2 cloves garlic*
2 red peppers	*Olive oil*
4 courgettes	

Cut the onions in small pieces and put into a heavy pan with about ¼ pint olive oil. Without peeling them, cut the aubergines into ½ inch slices and sprinkle with salt. Leave in a colander to drain away the juices. When the onions are soft, add the aubergines, sliced red peppers and courgettes. Cover and simmer for 30 minutes. Add chopped tomatoes and garlic and continue simmering until the tomatoes are completely soft and have blended into the mixture. Add a little more oil if necessary, but do not make the mixture mushy. Leave until cold and garnish with a little chopped parsley or basil.

SUMMER SLAW

1 dessertspoon made mustard	1 tablespoon finely chopped onion
4 fl oz salad dressing	¼ teaspoon caraway seeds
2 tablespoons single cream	1 lb finely shredded white cabbage
1 tablespoon vinegar	

Stir the mustard into the salad dressing with the cream and vinegar. Mix the onion and caraway seeds with the cabbage. Stir in the dressing very thoroughly so that all the cabbage is moistened.

CAULIFLOWER SALAD

1 lb freshly-cooked cauliflower sprigs	2 anchovies
1 hard-boiled egg yolk	1 tablespoon finely chopped onion
1 tablespoon tomato sauce	Chopped parsley
¼ pint of mayonnaise	

Put the cauliflower sprigs into a bowl. Sieve the egg yolk and mix it with tomato sauce and mayonnaise. Add finely chopped anchovies and onion. Mix this dressing with the cauliflower and garnish with chopped parsley. This is very good with beef.

FRENCH BEAN SALAD

2 lb cooked French beans	12 tablespoons salad oil
1 medium onion	Salt and pepper
4 tablespoons lemon juice	Chopped chives

The beans are best cut into chunks, not slivers. Chop the onion finely. Mix the beans and onion in a bowl. Shake the lemon juice, oil, salt and pepper together, and pour over the salad. Sprinkle with chopped chives.

TOMATO AND ONION SALAD

2 lb tomatoes	12 tablespoons salad oil
1 large onion	Salt and pepper
4 tablespoons wine vinegar	Chopped parsley or basil

Skin the tomatoes and cut them in thin slices. Peel the

onion and cut into very thin rings. Arrange in layers in a dish. Shake together the vinegar, oil, salt and pepper, and pour over the tomatoes and onion rings. Sprinkle with chopped parsley or basil.

CUCUMBER SALAD

1 cucumber	*¼ teaspoon salt*
2½ fl oz white wine vinegar	*White pepper*
1 tablespoon water	*Chopped parsley*
1 tablespoon caster sugar	

Slice the cucumber very thinly. Mix the vinegar, water, sugar, salt and pepper, and pour over the cucumber. Sprinkle with parsley. Cover and chill for about 3 hours before serving.

SPANISH POTATO SALAD

Small new potatoes	*Red peppers*
Olive oil	*Chives*
Garlic	

Cook the potatoes and drain them. While they are still warm, toss them in oil, well flavoured with crushed garlic or garlic powder. Garnish with chopped red peppers and chives. Canned red peppers can be used.

POTATO CRUNCH SALAD

2 tablespoons HP Fruity Sauce	*3-inch length cucumber, chopped*
4 tablespoons thick mayonnaise	*2 oz salted peanuts*
¼ pint whipped double cream	*1 level teaspoon chopped chives*
1 lb cooked new potatoes	*Salt and freshly ground black pepper*
2 dessert apples, cored and chopped	

Combine sauce, mayonnaise and cream. Slice or dice potatoes. Add to mayonnaise mixture with the rest of the ingredients.

DEVILLED POTATO AND CORN SALAD

1 lb boiled new potatoes
8 oz can sweetcorn, drained
4 tablespoons single or
  soured cream
1 tablespoon HP sauce
1 tablespoon chopped
  chives or spring onion
  tops

Cool and cut potatoes into ½-inch cubes and place in a large bowl with sweetcorn. Blend together single or soured cream and sauce. Pour over potatoes and corn and toss carefully to coat potatoes. Sprinkle with chives or spring onion tops.

ROSY RICE SALAD

6 oz cooked long grain
  rice
4 oz cooked peas
4-inch length cucumber,
  cut into ¼-inch cubes
3 chopped spring onions
2 chopped canned red
  peppers
Salt and pepper
Cucumber slices for garnish

Dressing

1 tablespoon lemon juice
¼ pint tomato juice
2 tablespoons Worcester-
  shire sauce
2 tablespoons salad oil
Salt and pepper

Mix together all ingredients, except garnish and dressing. Whisk dressing ingredients together and adjust seasoning. Stir sufficient dressing into salad to moisten, about 6-8 tablespoons. Leave 2 hours before serving. Garnish with cucumber slices. Keep extra dressing in a covered container in refrigerator. You could also use this to dress mixed green salad.

RICE AND PEPPER SALAD

8 oz long grain rice
2 green peppers
2 red peppers
3 firm tomatoes
1 medium onion
2 cloves garlic
2 tablespoons chopped
  parsley
Salt and pepper
Salad oil
Vinegar

Cook the rice and leave it until cool. Heat the peppers under the grill on the cooker until the skins begin to blacken. Peel off the skins and cut up the peppers, removing the seeds. Cut the flesh into small cubes. Skin the tomatoes and cut them into small pieces, removing the pips. Chop the onion into very small pieces. Crush the garlic and smear it around the salad bowl. Put in the rice, peppers, tomatoes and onions. Mix a dressing using three parts oil to one part vinegar (olive oil is best for this) and add salt and pepper. Pour over the rice and sprinkle with chopped parsley. Do not add the dressing until the salad is ready to serve.

FINISHING THE MEAL

After some simple barbecues, a selection of cheeses and a bowl of fresh fruit will be sufficient. A lot of people like a really sweet ending to an outdoor meal, though, and this is certainly a good idea for a party. It need not present problems as most of the dishes can be prepared beforehand and stored in a freezer or refrigerator. Other kinds of sweet endings can be cooked over the fire on skewers or in foil. The fire is also useful for keeping sweet sauces hot to serve over ice cream. Even if a full sweet course is not wanted, a sweet drink, perhaps with an ice cream float, may be welcome. Ideas are given in the section on 'Hot and Cold Drinks'.

It is best to avoid creamy mousses or soft puddings for barbecues as they tend to collapse in heat and do not look particularly attractive when served. Fruit is always popular, particularly in summer when the choice is so wide. The alternative is to serve rather rich cakes, or simpler cakes which can be cut into squares to serve with coffee. Ice cream is welcome on a hot night, and is all the better if there is a good choice of accompaniments.

SUMMER FRUIT BOWL

1 lb gooseberries	*4 oz raspberries*
4 oz redcurrants	*¼ pint water*
4 oz blackcurrants	*6 oz caster sugar*

Top and tail gooseberries and remove currants from stalks.

Put in water with sugar and bring slowly to the boil. Simmer very gently for 5 minutes without breaking the fruit. Cool and stir in raspberries.

SERVE-YOURSELF FRUIT SALAD

Melon chunks or balls	*Raspberries*
Pineapple	*Apricots*
Bananas	*Pears*
Apples	*Sugar*
Pears	*Orange Juice*
Oranges	*Chopped Nuts*
Grapes	*Liqueurs*
Strawberries	*Cream*

Choose a wide selection of fruit, from the suggestions above. The fruit can be fresh, canned or frozen, or a combination of all three. Put each kind of fruit into a separate bowl, and have a bowl of caster sugar, one of fresh orange juice, chopped nuts, a choice of complementary liqueurs (such as Kirsch or Maraschino), and pouring or whipped cream. Guests can assemble their own fruit salads, and finish them to taste with sugar, cream, and so on. It is best if apples, bananas and pears are cut and left in lemon juice to save discoloration. Oranges can be cut into slices or divided into sections.

SERVE-YOURSELF SUNDAES

1 or 2 flavours of ice cream	*Strawberries*
Sliced peaches	*Marshmallows*
Mandarin oranges	*Chopped nuts*
Sliced bananas	*Ice cream sauces*
Maraschino cherries	*Whipped cream*
Raspberries	*Small biscuits or wafers*

Use gallon or half-gallon containers of ice cream and store them in the freezer until just before use. Use an ice-cream scoop or rounded serving spoon and dip it in hot water to aid serving. Have vanilla for one ice cream flavour and strawberry or chocolate for the other. For a large party, have all three as well as orange and/or lemon water ice. Guests can prepare their own ice cream sundaes in bowls or tall glasses. Children like small jelly sweets, chocolate drops, raisins or hundreds-and-thousands to complete their sundaes. A wide range of bottled, canned and tubed ice cream sauces is available, or these may be home-made.

ORANGE AND BANANA SKEWERS

Oranges	*Golden syrup*
Bananas	*Chopped nuts*

Peel the oranges and cut them crosswise into 1½-inch slices. Peel the bananas and cut into 1½-inch slices. Warm a little golden syrup and brush it lightly on the banana pieces. Roll them in chopped nuts. Fill skewers with alternate pieces of orange and bananas and grill over a hot fire, turning often, until the nuts are just toasted.

MIXED FRUIT SKEWERS

Pineapple chunks	*Bananas*
Soaked prunes	*Maraschino cherries*
Eating apples	

Drain the syrup from the pineapple chunks. Remove the stones from the prunes which have been soaked overnight. Do not peel the apples, but cut them into wedges. Cut bananas into 1½-inch lengths. Fill the skewers with alternate pieces of pineapple, whole prunes, apple wedges, banana slices and cherries. Cook over hot fire for 5 minutes, turning often. If liked, brush fruit with a little honey and lemon juice during cooking.

SKEWERED MARSHMALLOWS

Marshmallows	*Chocolate sauce*

Put about eight marshmallows on each skewer. Heat the chocolate sauce very gently. Toast the marshmallows until they are soft inside and brown outside. Dip them into chocolate sauce and eat at once. The sauce and marshmallow mixture may be used over vanilla ice cream. Canned or bottled chocolate sauce is good for this, as it is usually rather syrupy.

FOILED BANANAS

4 large bananas	*Pinch of salt*
4 fl oz maple syrup	*1 tablespoon lemon juice*

Peel the bananas and save the peels. Put bananas into a bowl with the maple syrup, salt and lemon juice. Leave to stand for 15 minutes. Put the bananas back into their skins and wrap each one in foil. Put on the grill over medium heat for 15 minutes. Serve with the syrup mixture, and with ice cream if liked.

FOILED APPLES

1 apple per person	*Raisins*
Brown sugar	*Whipped cream*
Butter	

Remove cores from the apples and score the skin of each one around the middle. Place each apple on a square of heavy-duty foil, with a knob of butter in each, together with brown sugar and raisins. Put a knob of butter on top. Fold foil securely over the top. Cook for 45 minutes on grill over medium fire, turning once. Serve with cream.

STRAWBERRY CAKE

8 oz plain flour	*2 drops vanilla essence*
3 oz icing sugar	*1 lb strawberries*
4 oz butter	*4 oz redcurrant jelly*
2 egg yolks	*Whipped cream to taste*

Sift the flour and make a well in the centre. Put in the butter, sugar, egg yolks and essence, and mix to a smooth paste. Leave in a cool place for 30 minutes and then roll into a $\frac{1}{4}$-inch round. Prick all over and bake at 350°F (Gas Mark 4) for 25 minutes. Cool. Melt the redcurrant jelly and pour over cake, cover with strawberries cut in half. Brush the strawberries with remaining jelly. When set, decorate with whipped cream.

STRAWBERRY SHORTCAKE

1 lb strawberries	*Grated rind of 1 orange*
4 oz butter	*4 oz self-raising flour*
4 oz caster sugar	*Pinch of salt*
2 eggs	*Whipped cream to taste*

Hull the strawberries and wash them. Reserve a few for decoration, and crush the remaining berries, but do not mash them completely. Cream the butter and sugar and work in the eggs beaten with the orange peel, alternately with the sifted flour and salt. Put into two 7-inch greased and floured sandwich tins. Bake at 375°F (Gas Mark 5) for 30 minutes. Cool on a rack and sandwich together with crushed berries and whipped cream. Top with more cream and whole strawberries.

CHOCOLATE CAKE

4 oz margarine	*1 tablespoon cocoa*
5 oz caster sugar	*2 eggs*
4 oz self-raising flour	*1 tablespoon milk*

Slightly soften the margarine, put all the ingredients into a bowl and blend until creamy and smooth. Bake in two 7-inch tins at 350°F (Gas Mark 4) for 30 minutes. Cool and fill with icing made by blending together 6 oz icing sugar, 1 oz cocoa, 2 oz margarine and 2 dessertspoons hot water. Fill, put layers together and top the cake with more icing.

MOCHA CAKE

4 oz self-raising flour	*4 oz caster sugar*
Pinch of salt	*2 oz butter*
3 eggs	

Icing

4 oz butter	*3 oz chopped browned*
2 teaspoons coffee essence	*almonds*
6 oz icing sugar	

Sift together the flour and salt. Melt the butter slowly. Boil some water in a large saucepan, remove from heat and put a bowl over the hot water. Break the eggs into the bowl, add the sugar and whisk together for 5 minutes until pale and thick. Remove the bowl from the pan and continue whisking until cold. Add melted butter, flour and salt, and fold in until well mixed. Put into a lined 6-inch square tin. Bake at 350°F (Gas Mark 4) for 40 minutes. Cool. Make the icing by beating butter until soft and gradually working in the sugar until fluffy. Beat in the coffee essence. Cut the cake in half, spread with a thin layer of icing and put the halves together. Spread remaining icing on top of cake and sprinkle with nuts.

ICEBOX CAKE

6 oz icing sugar
4 oz butter
2 medium eggs

2 teaspoons grated lemon peel and 2 tablespoons lemon juice or 2 tablespoons cocoa and 1 teaspoon coffee essence
48 sponge finger biscuits

Cream icing sugar and butter together until light and fluffy, and work in eggs one at a time. Gradually beat in the peel and juice, or cocoa and coffee essence, and beat hard until fluffy and smooth. Cover a piece of cardboard with foil and on it place 12 biscuits, curved side down. On this put one-third of the creamed mixture. Arrange another layer of biscuits in the opposite direction, cover with more creamed mixture. Repeat the layers, ending with biscuits. Cover completely with foil, seal and freeze. To serve, unwrap and leave in the refrigerator for 3 hours. Cover completely with whipped cream (about ½ pint) and serve at once.

APPLE SHORTCAKE

6 oz self-raising flour
Pinch of salt
4 oz butter
3 oz caster sugar

1 egg
1 lb apples
Sugar for apples

Peel and slice the apples and cook with sugar to taste and

very little water. Cool. Sift flour and salt. Cream the butter
and sugar, and stir in the flour and beaten egg. Leave in a
cool place for 10 minutes to become firm. Grease a 7-inch
sandwich tin and put strips of greaseproof paper at right
angles across the base and up the sides so that the shortcake
can be lifted out easily. Line the base with greased greaseproof paper. Divide the pastry into halves, and roll out each
piece to a 7-inch round. Put one round in the tin, prick with
a fork and cover with apple. Cover with second round and
prick lightly. Bake at 325°F (Gas Mark 3) for 1 hour. Cool.
Dust with icing sugar.

SWEDISH APPLECAKE

3 oz brown breadcrumbs	*2 tablespoons brown sugar*
1 oz butter	*1 lb peeled cooking apples*

Gently fry the breadcrumbs in butter until golden brown.
Cook the apples in very little water until soft and sweeten to
taste. Sweeten the breadcrumbs with brown sugar. Arrange
alternate layers of crumbs and apples in a buttered foil dish,
beginning and ending with layers of crumbs. Press firmly into the dish and leave to cool. Turn out and serve with cream.

BROWNIES

8 oz granulated sugar	*4 oz melted butter or*
1½ oz cocoa	*margarine*
3 oz self-raising flour	*Optional—3 oz shelled*
½ teaspoon salt	*walnuts or seedless*
2 eggs	*raisins*
2 tablespoons creamy milk	

Stir together the sugar, cocoa, flour and salt. Beat the eggs
and milk and add to the dry mixture, together with the melted
fat. Stir in the broken walnuts or raisins if used. Pour into a
rectangular tin (about 8 x 12 inches) and bake at 350°F (Gas
Mark 4) for 30 minutes. Cool in the tin and cut in squares.

CHOCOLATE CRUMB CAKE

4 oz butter	*1 tablespoon golden syrup*
1 tablespoon sugar	*8 oz fine biscuit crumbs*
2 tablespoons cocoa	*4 oz plain chocolate*

Cream the butter and sugar and add the cocoa and syrup. Mix well and blend in biscuit crumbs. Press mixture into a greased foil tray about 1 inch deep. Chill for 5 hours. Cover with melted chocolate and cut in squares to serve.

BREAD

A varied selection of bread is useful for the barbecue. Soft rolls or baps can be warmed through or toasted for hamburgers or hot dogs, but they are also welcome for mopping up sauces. Crusty rolls, cottage loaves or French loaves are also good for this purpose, and for serving with cheese later. Serve crispbreads and bread sticks for nibbling with first courses.

Hot breads flavoured with garlic, herbs or cheese are particularly popular. They can be prepared in advance, wrapped in foil and stored in a freezer. They can be taken straight from the freezer to the barbecue, but the heating time should be doubled on the grill. Bread for heating must be wrapped securely in heavy-duty foil, and can be put right into the ashes or on the grill. It should be turned often and served very hot. You will need rather large quantities of these tempting breads; a 16-inch French loaf should be allowed for 4 people.

MUSTARD LOAF

1 French loaf	*2 tablespoons chopped*
2 oz butter	*parsley*
2 tablespoons French	*1 small onion*
mustard	

Split the loaf diagonally in 2-inch chunks, without quite cutting to the bottom. Cream the butter with mustard, parsley and finely chopped onion. Spread the butter mixture between the slices, and wrap the loaf in foil. Place on hot grill for 20 minutes.

HERB BREAD CUBES
4 thick bread slices
2 oz melted butter
1 tablespoon chopped fresh herbs

Cut the bread into cubes. Toss in butter and herbs. Put into a thick frying pan and stir over fire until hot and beginning to brown on the edges. Serve with grilled meats.

HOT CRISP STICKS
Bridge rolls
Melted butter
Poppy seeds or sesame seeds or chopped nuts or Parmesan cheese

Cut the rolls in lengthwise quarters. Brush them all over with melted butter. Roll them in poppy seeds, sesame seeds, chopped nuts or cheese. Put on baking tray over fire and turn often until crisp and golden.

HERB LOAF
1 French loaf
4 oz butter
2 tablespoons chopped chives
2 tablespoons chopped tarragon

Split the loaf diagonally in 2-inch chunks, without quite cutting to the bottom. Cream the butter with chives and tarragon. Spread the butter mixture between slices, and wrap the loaf in foil. Place on hot grill for 20 minutes.

GARLIC LOAF
1 French loaf
4 oz butter
3 cloves garlic

Split the loaf diagonally in 2-inch chunks, without quite cutting to the bottom. Cream the butter with the crushed garlic cloves. Spread the butter mixture between slices, and wrap the loaf in foil. Place on hot grill for 20 minutes.

GARLIC BUTTER SLICES

1 French loaf
4 oz butter

2 cloves garlic

Cut the bread in 1½-inch slices. Melt the butter in a baking dish and add minced garlic. Dip both sides of each slice in the melted butter. Leave to stand for 10 minutes. Put on a baking tray, and place over warm grill for 15 minutes.

PARSLEY ROLLS

4 bread rolls
2 oz butter

2 tablespoons chopped parsley
1 teaspoon lemon juice

Split the rolls crosswise. Cream the butter with the parsley and lemon juice. Spread the butter mixture on the rolls and put them together again. Wrap in foil and place on hot grill for 20 minutes.

ONION SLICES

1 French loaf
4 oz butter

4 tablespoons chopped spring onion tops

Cut the loaf in half horizontally. Mix the butter and onion tops and spread on the cut sides of the bread. Slash each half loaf in 2-inch diagonal slices, not quite cutting through the bottom crust. Wrap in foil and place on hot grill for 20 minutes.

FRENCH ONION BREAD

1 French loaf
4 oz butter
1 tablespoon chopped parsley

1 onion
Salt and pepper

Split the loaf diagonally in inch-thick slices, not quite through to the bottom. Cream the butter with parsley and spread generously between the slices. Cut the onion in thin slices and slip them between the bread slices. Sprinkle with salt and pepper. Wrap in foil and place over hot grill for 25 minutes.

BARBECUE BREAD

1 round wholemeal loaf
4 oz butter
2 heaped tablespoons grated cheese
½ teaspoon Worcestershire sauce

1 tablespoon prepared mustard
1 tablespoon finely chopped onion or parsley

Cut the loaf in ½-inch slices. Cream the butter and work in the cheese, sauce, mustard and onion or parsley. Spread the slices and put the loaf together, then cut in half. Wrap in foil and place over hot grill for 25 minutes. Serve from the foil with the top turned back.

BARBECUED BREAD STICKS

Italian bread sticks (Grissini)
Melted butter

Tabasco sauce
Paprika
Garlic

Put the bread sticks on a double thickness of aluminium foil. Season the butter with a few drops of Tabasco sauce, a dash of paprika and minced garlic to taste. Brush the bread sticks with the butter. Wrap securely in foil and place on hot grill for 5 minutes, turning frequently.

ITALIAN BREAD

1 French loaf
3 oz butter
3 oz Parmesan cheese
1 tablespoon olive oil

2 tablespoons finely chopped parsley
½ teaspoon basil
1 clove garlic
Salt and pepper to taste

Split the loaf diagonally in inch-thick slices, not quite through to the bottom. Cream the butter and work in cheese, oil, parsley, basil, chopped garlic and seasoning. Spread generously between the slices. Wrap in foil and place over hot grill for 25 minutes.

GARLIC BREAD

1 French loaf	*4 oz butter*
2 cloves garlic	*Salt and pepper*

Peel the garlic and crush it with the flat blade of a knife. Mix with the butter and leave to stand for 15 minutes. Season to taste. Cut the loaf of bread in diagonal slices about 1½-2 inches thick, not cutting right through the bottom of the loaf. Spread the garlic butter between the slices. Wrap in foil. Heat on grill over hot fire for 15 minutes and serve hot.

HOT AND COLD DRINKS

For a small family or party barbecue, drinks can be very simple. Adults like beer, cider or wine, followed by large cups of coffee. Children like milk or milk shakes, fresh fruit drinks or bottled minerals. It is important that drinks are fairly strong to cope with the strongly-flavoured barbecue food, and it would be pointless to serve vintage wines for such an occasion.

For large parties, a preliminary drink of spirits, a chilled aperitif, or a tomato-based cocktail, is a good idea. A mixed cider, fruit or wine cup is also suitable for a party on a hot night or you could serve glasses of iced tea or coffee. If the weather turns chilly, a hot punch or coffee spiked with spirits and spices are very popular. Children like hot chocolate. These hot drinks can be easily kept warm at the side of the grill, or can be freshly heated when the main course has been cooked.

It is important that cold drinks should be very cold. They can stand in a bath or bucket of ice (make large blocks of ice in foil trays or polythene bags in the freezer). If ice is put into bowls of wine or cider cup, it is better to use a large block rather than small cubes which melt quickly and dilute drinks. Drinks which have been mixed in a blender in the house can be stored in a chilled vacuum flask, which can be lightly shaken before serving.

Cold drinks keep colder longer if glasses are chilled in the refrigerator for 15 minutes before serving. They can also be 'frosted' by dipping the rims of glasses into cold water and then into caster sugar.

TOMATO COCKTAIL

1 lb fresh or canned
tomatoes
½ teaspoon salt
Pepper

1 teaspoon sugar
6 ice cubes
3 drops Worcestershire
sauce

Put all the ingredients into a blender and blend on maximum speed for 30 seconds. Strain and serve at once.

TOMATO AND ORANGE COCKTAIL

1 pint tomato juice
½ pint orange juice

Pinch of salt
1 dessertspoon sugar

Put all the ingredients into a blender and blend on maximum speed for 25 seconds. Chill for 1 hour before serving.

VERMOUTH CASSIS

1 large bottle dry French
Vermouth
3 liqueur glasses Cassis

1 siphon soda water
Crushed ice

Pour Vermouth and Cassis over the ice, and immediately before serving add soda water. Serve well chilled.

SANGRIA

2 bottles red wine
1 bottle lemonade
1 liqueur glass brandy

Handful of fresh fruit in
season (apple, orange or
strawberries)
Crushed ice

Pour the red wine and lemonade over ice. Add the brandy and fruit. Serve cold

VIN ROSÉ CUP

1 bottle vin rosé   *1 sliced peach*
1 bottle lemonade   *Ice*
4 dessertspoons honey   *Sugar*
4 slices lemon

Mix chilled ingredients together and pour over ice in bowl. Stir honey to ensure that it is properly blended into the wine. Add sugar to taste if necessary. Serve cold.

SPICE ISLAND

1 bottle red Burgundy   *Soft brown sugar to taste*
4 tablespoons brandy   *Crushed ice*
1 pint ginger beer

Dissolve brown sugar in brandy, and then add red Burgundy and crushed ice. Allow to stand for at least an hour, and just before serving add the ginger beer.

BEAUJOLAIS BOWL

1 bottle Beaujolais   *4 pineapple slices*
2 large bottles lemonade   *Soda water to taste*
2 liqueur glasses   *Granulated sugar to taste*
  Maraschino   *Sprigs of mint*
Peel of 1 lemon

Chill all ingredients in the refrigerator. Pour Beaujolais and lemonade into bowl. Add lemon peel and soda water to taste. Add sugar to taste, and sprigs of mint.

FROZEN SUNSHINE

3 bottles dry white wine   *1 pint lemonade*
¼ bottle Cognac   *Sugar to taste*
9 tablespoons Benedictine   *Block of ice*
½ lb cut pineapple, either
  fresh or tinned

Soak the pineapple in brandy for 15 minutes. Add well-chilled white wine, lemonade and Benedictine. Leave for half an hour in refrigerator or cool place and then add sugar to taste.

CIDER CUP

2 quarts cider	1 pint pineapple juice
½ bottle orange squash	1 wineglass sherry
½ bottle lemon squash	Dash of Angostura bitters

Mix together the cider, squashes, pineapple juice, sherry and bitters. Leave to stand for 2 hours. Pour over ice and decorate with mint and fruit to taste.

PINEAPPLE PUNCH

5 oz sugar	2¼ pints unsweetened pine-apple juice
½ pint water	
12 inch cinnamon stick	½ pint orange juice
12 whole cloves	¼ pint lemon juice
	1½ pints ginger ale

Mix the sugar, water, cinnamon and cloves and put into a pan. Cover, simmer for 15 minutes and strain. Mix with the pineapple, orange and lemon juices and chill. Just before serving, pour over plenty of ice and carefully pour in ginger ale down the side of the punch bowl.

ICED COFFEE (1)

1½ oz ground coffee	Milk
1 pint water	Sugar

Pour boiling water on to the coffee, stir well and leave to stand for 4 minutes. Strain into a non-metal container, cover tightly and chill in the refrigerator for no longer than 3 hours. See that the milk is also kept in the refrigerator. Just before serving, add milk and sugar to taste. Usually 2 lumps of sugar will sweeten ½ pint iced coffee. The proportions of milk and coffee can be varied to taste. For a foamy top, mix in a blender or with an egg whisk. Serve in tall glasses with straws.

ICED COFFEE (2)

Make up coffee as in Iced Coffee (1) and pour into ice cube

trays. Freeze until solid. Make up a second batch of coffee and mix with milk and sugar. Fill glasses half-full with coffee ice cubes, and top up with fresh coffee.

ICED COFFEE (3)
Make up double-strength coffee by using half the amount of water in Iced Coffee (1). Mix this fresh coffee with an equal amount of milk, sweeten to taste, and pour over plain ice cubes.

ICED COFFEE (4)
Make up coffee with instant coffee powder, using a double quantity of powder dissolved in very little hot water. Top up with cold milk, or equal proportions of cold milk and water, and finish with sugar and ice cubes.

ICED COFFEE CREAM
Instant coffee powder   *Sugar to taste*
Creamy milk   *5 fl oz double cream*

Make coffee with hot milk, sweetening to taste. Cool and then chill for 1 hour in the refrigerator. Pour into tall glasses with an ice cube in each and top with spoonfuls of whipped cream.

ICED TEA
Hot, extra-strong tea   *Sugar*
Ice cubes   *Lemon slices*

Make the tea (choose a fragrant tea if possible) and leave to settle for 5 minutes. Strain into tall glasses half-filled with ice cubes. Serve with sugar to taste and lemon slices.

FRESH LEMONADE
4 large lemons   *1 dessertspoon tartaric acid*
2 lb sugar   *1 quart water*
1 teaspoon oil of lemon

Squeeze the lemons over the sugar in a basin. Add the oil

and acid and pour on the boiling water. Stir well until the sugar has dissolved. Cool and bottle. Dilute to taste.

BASIC MILK SHAKE (1 SERVING)

¼ pint chilled milk
1 tablespoon ice cream
Sugar and flavouring to taste

Put all the ingredients in a blender, and blend on maximum speed for 30 seconds. Flavour with commercial milk shake syrup; 2 drops vanilla or other essence; 1 teaspoon powdered coffee; 1 teaspoon drinking chocolate; 1 tablespoon jam; 1 tablespoon soft fruit.

COFFEE ICE CREAM SHAKE (6 SERVINGS)

1½ pints chilled milk
8 oz vanilla ice cream
½ pint chilled black coffee
2 tablespoons sugar
8 ice cubes

Put all the ingredients into a blender and blend on maximum speed for 1 minute. This could be used instead of a sweet course.

MULLED CIDER

3 oz soft brown sugar
Pinch of salt
4 pints cider
½ teaspoon whole allspice
½ teaspoon whole cloves
3 inch cinnamon sticks
Pinch of nutmeg
Twist of orange peel

Mix the sugar, salt and cider. Tie the spices into a muslin bag and suspend in a saucepan with the cider. Bring slowly to the boil and simmer with a lid on for 20 minutes. Remove spices and serve cider hot with a twist of orange peel in each glass.

HOT BUTTERED CIDER

3 pints cider
3 tablespoons brown sugar
3 tablespoons butter
½ pint light rum

Bring the cider and sugar to the boil in a thick saucepan

over a low heat. Remove from the heat and stir in the butter. When this has melted, stir in the rum, and serve at once.

SPICED CIDER PUNCH

1 quart cider
8 cloves
1 cinnamon stick, broken
2 pieces mace
Little grated nutmeg

1 lemon, thinly peeled
1 orange, thinly peeled
¼ pint water
1 oz brown sugar
Cinnamon sticks for serving

Put the cloves, cinnamon stick, mace, nutmeg, fruit peel, water, and sugar into a small saucepan. Bring to the boil slowly and simmer gently for 15 minutes. Strain into a large saucepan and add the cider. Heat until foaming and nearly boiling. Serve immediately in warmed glasses with a cinnamon stick in each.

BUTTERED RUM

6 lumps sugar
1 tablespoon hot water
½ teaspoon ground allspice

½ teaspoon ground cloves
8 fl oz rum
6 teaspoons fresh butter

Dissolve the sugar in the water. Add all the other ingredients except the butter. Stir well and pour into six hot mugs. Add boiling water to taste and a knob of butter in each mug. Serve hot.

HOT TEA PUNCH

2 pints freshly-made tea
½ pint dark rum
3 tablespoons butter
4 oz sugar

Thin rind of ½ lemon
¼ teaspoon grated nutmeg
4 fl oz brandy
Lemon slices

Put tea, rum, butter, sugar, lemon rind, and nutmeg into a saucepan and heat gently. In a separate small saucepan, heat the brandy. When the tea mixture is hot, ignite the brandy and pour it into the tea mixture. Serve at once in small mugs with lemon slices.

BORGIA COFFEE

1 pint hot fresh coffee
1 pint hot milky chocolate
2 tablespoons double cream
*1 tablespoon grated orange
peel*

Mix together coffee and chocolate. Pour into mugs. Float
a dessertspoon of cream on each, and sprinkle with orange
peel. This drink may also be served chilled, topped with
lightly whipped cream and grated chocolate.

IRISH COFFEE

Freshly-made strong coffee
Irish whiskey
Sugar lumps
Thick cream

Put sugar lumps into mugs or Irish coffee glasses (some
people may not care for sugar, which can be omitted). Pour
on whiskey to taste. Fill with hot coffee. Pour on cream over
the back of a teaspoon so that it floats on the coffee. Serve at
once.

COFFEE GROG

*2 pints freshly-made strong
coffee*
6 sugar lumps
1 lemon
6 cloves
1 cinnamon stick
¼ pint light rum

Keep the coffee hot. Rub the sugar over the lemon rind
and put into a bowl. Add the cloves, cinnamon stick and
thinly-peeled rind of half the lemon. Warm the rum and
pour on to the sugar. Stir well and add to the coffee. Bring
just to the boil and serve at once.

HOT CHOCOLATE

2 pints milk
*4 tablespoons drinking
chocolate powder*
1 cinnamon stick
8 marshmallows

Heat the milk in a heavy saucepan over a low heat. Stir in
the chocolate powder with the cinnamon stick. When ready
to serve, pour into mugs and top with marshmallows.

PART FOUR

Party Barbecues

PLANNING FOR LARGE NUMBERS

A barbecue party is a wonderful way of entertaining a lot of people without turning the house upside down. Far more people can be accommodated and fed, even in a small garden, than in the average room, without damage and without the awful clearing-up afterwards. A party for 20 or 200 can be run with ease, and without vast stocks of expensive equipment, but it needs very careful planning.

PLANNING THE MENU

A form of buffet or help-yourself meal is the most popular kind, so that people mix easily and the cook, or cooks, can concentrate on the fire and skilful cooking without having to worry about serving food as well. Suit the meal to the weather; if the day is a little cold, people will crowd around the fire and want more cooked foods and spicy sauces. On a hot day, cool salads and fruit dishes will be most popular, with simply cooked meat. Also try to suit the type of guests. Children like a lot of simple finger food such as sausages and chicken drumsticks, marshmallows to toast, and plenty to drink. A small party of people who know each other well will enjoy steaks or chicken, a good salad, some special bread, and a delicious sweet course. A large party of people who know each other less will benefit from a wide menu with plenty of selection, and often budget-price foods must be chosen in preference to steaks or chops, and expensive accompaniments. If there are any doubts about people's tastes, keep main items simple, but provide plenty of sauces, unusual breads and salads for the more adventurous.

Try to serve food which is easy to handle, and keep to one kind of meat, unless you want to serve an accompaniment such as sausages or bacon with poultry. Add a salad and/or one or two vegetables, some kind of bread, and a sweet course. Too much choice can be confusing and result in food wastage.

QUANTITIES

Appetites are usually large in the open air when everyone is relaxed. For the meat course, allow 1½ to 2 helpings for each person. For each helping, allow 4 oz meat without fat or 6-8 oz fatty meat. If you are serving a roasting joint with the bone in, allow 8-12 oz per helping, and 1 lb of spareribs. A single chicken piece, 1 large chop, 2 large or 4 small sausages would be an average helping. Allow double quantities of salads, vegetables and bread. About 8 oz potatoes, 1 bread roll or 2 chunks of French bread is the usual quantity needed for each person.

Order drinks of all kinds generously. In cooler weather, spirit-based drinks will be the most popular; in very hot weather, the demand will be for beer, cider and soft drinks. Be generous also in the amount of coffee allowed, planning to serve large mugs rather than small after-dinner cups. For 20 people allow 1 lb ground coffee to 6 pints of water and 6 pints of milk.

EQUIPMENT FOR COOKING AND SERVING

For a large party, two or more barbecues may be necessary. If these can be borrowed from friends, it is a good idea to ask the owners to help with the cooking, as they will know best how to manage their own equipment. An extra fire or barbecue is useful to help keep food hot, or candle-warmers can be used on serving tables. Some large barbecues have racks for holding extra cooked food while further stocks are being prepared. The range of food can be extended, and the fire fully used if some food is cooked in foil parcels, and on skewers, as well as directly on the grill.

In addition to the barbecues, it is a good idea to have a food preparation table within easy reach of the cooks, to hold the extra supplies of uncooked meat, foil parcels, prepared skewers, etc., which can be kept ready on metal or plastic trays, covered with mesh domes, or with muslin.

A long serving table is essential to hold salads, breads, sweet courses, cutlery and plates. Keep this separate from any cooking or drinking arrangements, and see that food can be kept covered until required. Use paper plates and bowls for eating, and plastic cutlery for large numbers, and have large bins or boxes ready to take the dirty plates and food rubbish.

Arrange a drinks table away from the main food area so that people do not get in the way of the cooking. If possible, use transparent plastic glasses to avoid dangerous breakages, as glasses tend to be left around where people are walking or sitting. Keep supplies of ice in a tin bath or baby's bath for cooling bottles.

Plenty of rugs and cushions are useful for those who don't mind eating at floor level. Those who object will welcome small tables and chairs (these can usually be hired from your local pub for a large party, as can trestle tables for serving).

SERVING HINTS

Try to keep hot things hot and cold things cold. Food prepared in the kitchen can be wrapped in layers of newspaper or put into a straw-lined box to keep warm. Vacuum flasks can be used to keep sauces hot or liquids cold. Casseroles or heatproof dishes can be used at the side of the barbecue unit to keep accompaniments warm. Salads and other prepared foods should be chilled several hours before serving and will then retain their coolness longer.

Carry out plates, glasses and other equipment in a clothes basket or similar easily portable carrier. This can then be kept near the barbecue for carrying back items after the party.

Always keep some food in reserve for second helpings, such as a spare bowl of salad, extra sweet course, loaves of bread, and bowls of sauces, and do not bring them out until everyone has had their first helping served. Try not to have too many small bowls and plates for serving food, as this causes congestion at the table and slows up service. It is best to have two large bowls or plates of each type of food, e.g. salad, so that service can start at two places along the table.

Try to prepare as much food as possible beforehand when large numbers have to be served. Salads, sweet courses and soft drinks can be prepared hours in advance. Garlic bread and other foil-wrapped foods can also be prepared, and kebabs strung on skewers. Burgers can be formed and stacked with waxed paper between them so that they can be quickly handled for cooking. Sausages can be cooked under the grill or in the oven and brought out to the barbecue in foil-lined oven trays to keep hot near the fire. Dishes which need some initial preparation should be partly-cooked in the kitchen, and then taken to the barbecue for finishing with sauce. Not only does this mean that food can be served quickly and efficiently, but also that it can be fully cooked. There is nothing worse than hanging over a barbecue fire waiting for food to finish a long slow cooking, when people are queuing up hungrily and probably drinking too much while they wait.

SETTING THE SCENE

It is not really enough to plonk a barbecue in the garden and ask a few friends in, hoping for a super party. Apart from planning the meal and the means of cooking it, it is important to set the scene for the party to encourage the right mood in the guests. In the same way that a dinner party needs flowers or some other kind of table centre, and the appropriate china, silver and glass, so the outdoor party needs its own special atmosphere. This comes down to the basics of an attractive setting, comfortable temperature, cunning lighting and protection from marauding insects.

CREATING AN ATMOSPHERE

For the sake of convenience, it is a good idea to try and have the barbecue reasonably near the house, either on a lawn or terrace. Not only does this make serving easier, but it also means that the house and its lighting can form part of the setting. If all the house lights are on as a background to the party, they will give enough illumination to work by, and can be supplemented with other decorative lighting. Use candles in glass lanterns for table lights, or hang them in trees (but, of course, do not use naked candles). Night-lights in jam jars can also provide lighting, and are useful to put at the sides of steps or along pathways to guide strangers. Hurricane lights or storm lanterns run on oil make useful and safe emergency lights, and one or two large torches can be handy for the cooks. Coloured flares on long sticks will burn for a couple of hours and look dramatic, as well as lighting up driveways or dark spots.

KEEPING WARM OR COOL

Evenings can turn very cold, and a bonfire makes a marvellous and decorative focus for a barbecue party in a large garden. Chairs or benches can be arranged nearby as a lot of people like to sit by a fire as the evening goes on. There is an added bonus as paper and food rubbish can be burned quickly, leaving little to clear up the next day. Make sure the fire is a really large one, built in a Guy Fawkes pyramid fashion and consisting of wood, not just garden rubbish.

If the night is very hot, people may be looking for something to cool them down, and running water or a fountain will look and sound refreshing. Even a garden sprinkler at a little distance from the party will help to cool the atmosphere.

KEEPING AWAY INSECTS

Lights and fires and food will attract all sorts of flying and crawling insects. Keep an aerosol spray handy against attack, and keep food well-covered. Have a bottle of insect repellent available for sensitive skins which need protection, and a first-aid box for those who suffer bites or stings.

ENTERTAINMENT

The right sort of music helps to create a relaxing atmosphere at a barbecue. A record player in the background can be used, with records chosen to suit the age of the guests and the mood of the party; some parties benefit from stimulating music, others from something soft and soothing. A guitarist and/or folk singer is right for an outdoor party. If no friend is available to play, it is worth approaching a local school, college or club to see if there is anyone who wants to earn some money and a free supper and drinks. Theatre ticket agencies often run an entertainment section for hiring professional performers, and for a charity function, this is money well spent.

Also for a charity, or a large private party, fireworks combine well with a barbecue. Large boxes of party-size fireworks, set-pieces, etc., are obtainable on order at any time of the year from shops which normally stock fireworks in November. Various types of display can be chosen, and in the summer one which incorporates only airborne fireworks is particularly successful. Ask a couple of very responsible men to handle the display, and be sure they look at the selection and prepare the ground some hours ahead, as many of the larger fireworks need special posts put up, or pits dug.

Another popular pastime on a relaxed evening is 'playing the machines'. A selection of old bagatelles, skittles, fruit machines or end-of-the-pier machines can be collected together from friends or junk shops, or they can be hired. These are amusing and can also raise useful cash for charity.

SPECIAL OCCASIONS

A straightforward barbecue is always fun, but sometimes the

party is for a very special occasion, either private or public, and a little extra effort must be made. When raising money for charity, it is particularly important to have a theme which can be widely advertised to bring in more guests and more money.

A BARBECUE PLUS

This can be for private or public parties, and the 'plus' can be altered to suit the budget and the occasion. The food can be basically simple—chicken pieces, sausages, burgers, with one good barbecue sauce, long crusty loaves, cheese and fresh fruit, or a fruit salad or gâteau as a sweet course. The additions, which should be kept secret from the guests until they arrive, consist of such things as a bonfire, fireworks, a group of musicians, a barn to dance in, swimming facilities, or a scavenge hunt with prizes

OX, LAMB OR HOG ROAST

Roasting a beast in the open air is becoming an increasingly popular way to raise money for charity. An *ox roast* is a fairly complicated undertaking and should be organised by a butcher or professional roaster (they are often available through local American or British army units). It is a time-consuming business, and there must be a certain gamble with the weather for about 48 hours.

A lamb or sucking pig is best for home barbecuing, but it is not wise to tackle this sort of party without some experience of fire-making and of barbecue cooking. A large open fire with a tripod arrangement is necessary, or a very large barbecue with a grill.

A lamb should be between 30-35 lb weight for comfortable cooking and serving, and this quantity will feed about 50 people (8-12 oz per serving which allows for bones and wastage). Prepare the lamb by splitting it in half lengthwise and inserting a few pieces of garlic under the skin. Add rosemary or thyme for fragrance, and baste with red wine during the cooking. If a tripod is available, the lamb is best enclosed in a stainless steel basket, but it can be cooked on a grill about 15 inches from the fire. Turn the meat frequently and allow three times longer cooking on the bone side than on the skin side, cooking for a total of 20 minutes per lb. To serve, cut the meat in bite-size pieces or carve into slices, depending on the help available for cutting and serving.

A pig for barbecuing is best at the sucking stage, under 20 lb and 1 lb weight should be allowed per serving. The pig should be cooked in the same way as a lamb, but without basting, and is most easily tackled if cut in half. The skin should be scored and rubbed with plenty of salt to give crisp crackling. Allow 25 minutes per lb and serve in the same way as the lamb.

HARVEST SUPPER

The weather may be a bit cooler at the end of harvest, but a barbecue is an ideal way to celebrate a successful summer. Everyone will appreciate a warming bonfire and a hearty meal. Sausages, ham or bacon and poultry are best for a simple meal, but a lamb or pig would be appropriate too. Plenty of jacket potatoes and corn on the cob make good accompaniments, and tomatoes will be cheap for salads. Freshly-baked crusty bread, English cheeses and apple pies finish the meal well. Beer, cider or a wine cup are ideal thirst-quenching drinks for this meal.

HAWAIIAN FEAST

This is good for a really hot summer evening. Have masses of flowers for decoration, and string some flower heads on strong thread with a darning needle to make garlands. Serve chicken or pork, preferably with a pineapple or sweet and sour basting sauce. Seafood would make a good first course, and fruit or ices as a sweet course. Fruit punch spiked with rum and well-iced is the best drink.

CHILDREN'S BARBECUES

Barbecue parties are very popular with children, particularly combined with swimming. *For children up to 12*, be sure there are responsible adults in charge of the cooking and serving, and any entertainment. Some form of sports or competitive games can be arranged. Serve familiar foods like sausages, burgers, fish fingers, and plenty of baked beans. Salads are not too popular at this age, but jacket potatoes or bowls of crisps go down well. Ices are the most popular sweet course, and do-it-yourself sundaes can be prepared by quite small children. A large chocolate cake is messy but usually enjoyed. The best drinks are fruit squashes or bottled minerals, well-chilled, and served with straws. *For children over 12*, much less supervision is required, as they can usually tackle their own cooking. It is a good idea to pre-cook some of the food, and prepare salads, etc., in advance. They will enjoy chicken pieces or minute steaks, and, of course, sausages and burgers. Jacket potatoes, crisps and corn-on-the-cob are good accompaniments, and a spicy barbecue sauce will be liked by some. They will also enjoy salads, crusty bread and cheese, and fresh fruit. Older ones will not worry much about a pudding. According to age, bottled minerals, cider, beer or a fruit cup are popular drinks. For a party of this age, a record player or a guitarist will create a party atmosphere, but the children will not care for any organised entertainment.

Index

INDEX